THE
FOURTH WIFE OF
Aliyar Bey

THE
FOURTH WIFE OF
Aliyar Bey

Hélène Zulgadar;
Nandita Jhaveri-Menon

AuthorHouse™ UK
1663 Liberty Drive
Bloomington, IN 47403 USA
www.authorhouse.co.uk
Phone: 0800.197.4150

© 2014 Hélène Zulgadar; Nandita Jhaveri-Menon. All rights reserved.

No part of this book may be reproduced, stored in a retrieval system, or transmitted by any means without the written permission of the author.

Published by AuthorHouse 11/14/2014

ISBN: 978-1-4969-9413-4 (sc)

Any people depicted in stock imagery provided by Thinkstock are models, and such images are being used for illustrative purposes only.
Certain stock imagery © Thinkstock.

Because of the dynamic nature of the Internet, any web addresses or links contained in this book may have changed since publication and may no longer be valid. The views expressed in this work are solely those of the author and do not necessarily reflect the views of the publisher, and the publisher hereby disclaims any responsibility for them.

Contents

Chapter 1	Birth of a Partnership	1
Chapter 2	The Cossack's Daughter	11
Chapter 3	A Joyless Marriage	25
Chapter 4	Algeria	36
Chapter 5	The Formation of the French Foreign Legion	48
Chapter 6	Val De Grâce	56
Chapter 7	To the East	71
Chapter 8	A break from Hélène's story and a discovery	82
Chapter 9	Persia becomes Iran	99
Chapter 10	Hélène continues her account	113
Chapter 11	Ninon	125
Chapter 12	Tehran	136
Chapter 13	Queen and Shahbanou	149
Chapter 14	Le Bistrot	160
Chapter 15	Southern Interlude	174
Chapter 16	Iranbarite	185
Chapter 17	Dizine	197
Chapter 18	Le Bavaria	206
Chapter 19	Gathering Clouds and a Final Parting	214
Chapter 20	The Narrator returns to La Métairie	219
Chapter 21	Further Revelations	228

ACKNOWLEDGEMENTS

My thanks to Marie-Aude and Gilles Serra, for encouragement and for coming to see me wherever I was at the time; to Khodadad Farman-farmaian for taking the time to talk to me about Zulu, and for lunch; to Karin Stephen for sharing her memories of the Zulgadars and of Iran; to Brigitte Nicolas for her notes on the Zulgadars; to Malek and Ilkhan Zelli, to Farida and Mahmoud Haerizadeh, and Abolmajid Majidi, for taking such an interest as the writing progressed. And, of course, to my sons and their wives for believing I could finish this book.

Nandita Jhaveri-Menon,
Cyprus 2014

Chapter 1

BIRTH OF A PARTNERSHIP

France and Spain, 2003–04

The bunch of flowers I clutched wilted rapidly in the late afternoon heat. I had spent an unsuccessful hour scrambling around a cemetery looking for a grave, feeling quite foolish as I peered at headstones. Exasperated and frustrated, I was also cross with the two old women who were the reason for this expedition. I sat down on a bench to catch my breath and reflect on how and why I was here. The why was short and easy to answer – I had allowed myself to be manipulated, no doubt about that. The how takes a bit longer.

Early in spring 2003, I resigned from my job as an in-house translator with a multinational company and decided to spend a few months away from my usual haunts. Mathilde Lebrun, a family friend, graciously offered me the use of Les Glycines, a converted barn on the edge of her property near Bordeaux. She herself occupied the main house, La Métairie. I had never visited her there, as my parents and I had always met her in Paris.

I arrived to occupy it two weeks later. The transformed building in front of me looked nothing like the barn it once was, with its front covered in the wisteria for which it was named. Mathilde was away, and her housekeeper settled me in. Three spacious, high-ceilinged rooms comprised Les Glycines, along with a kitchen giving onto a patio with a border of herbs along one side and the grounds of the estate stretching out beyond a cotoneaster hedge. To my relief, the kitchen and bathroom were modern and well-equipped.

A few days after I had unpacked and done the round of the village shops, Mathilde rang to say she was back and invited me to lunch the next day. It had been some years since I had last seen Mathilde, and my youthful memory of her was of a butterfly, always in motion and dressed in bright colours. There had been no mention of a lunch party when I had confirmed my arrival, and the short notice led me to suspect I was filling in for a last-minute defection. Though I was in no mood to attend a party, courtesy demanded I accept; she was, after all, my hostess. I had no other acquaintances in the area and could hardly plead a prior engagement. There was nothing for it but to present myself at noon the following day.

In a spacious drawing room where French windows gave onto a broad paved terrace and an expanse of lawn sloping down to a small stream, I was introduced to a colourless gathering quite unlike Mathilde herself. She remained much as I remembered her, dressed in vivid colours, still strikingly attractive, with deep auburn hair and an animated manner. The one exception in this lacklustre collection of stodgy local worthies was a willowy woman who looked to be a little older than Mathilde and was introduced as Hélène. Her fading blond hair was caught in a chignon with a black bow and she wore a chic suit with a slim skirt, beautifully cut in a 1950's style. She had, no doubt, turned many heads when she was younger and now held the attention of a couple of gentlemen who hovered about her. The conversation may have been uninspiring, but Mathilde kept a good table and the atmosphere over lunch was convivial.

Knowing that Mathilde rarely drove herself further than the neighbouring village, I reciprocated later that week by inviting her to a reputed country restaurant some twenty minutes away. A couple of hours spent in the company of an ageing beauty can be taxing, even if one likes her, so I asked whether her friend Hélène would care to join us – *two* ageing beauties who were apparently on friendly terms could, I hoped, spend a few hours in each other's company without becoming competitive.

As we drove to Hélène's house on the edge of a nearby village, Mathilde told me that Hélène had grown up in Paris where her parents had settled after leaving what became the Soviet Union in the 1920s. She had been a model, recounted Mathilde, when she met her late husband, Aliyar, with whom she went to Iran. He had been an inveterate womaniser and she had been his fourth wife. The couple owned a popular restaurant in Tehran when Mathilde and her late husband, Albert, had made their acquaintance in the 1970s. Albert was heading a construction project in Iran.

'You remember I spent five years in Iran, and Albert stayed on for another year? Tehran was quite cosmopolitan then. I used to accompany Albert when he had meetings there, and sometimes I went alone for a bit of shopping and just to get away from the sticks.'

'Sounds rather dull.'

'Not at all. I enjoyed my years there. The people are hospitable, but being stuck at the site for weeks could get quite tedious, with no entertainment other than the bland conversation of the company wives or the men's shop talk, which was even worse. Hélène and Aliyar were good hosts in both their professional and private lives. Their restaurant was one of the places to be seen, and the bar was like a club – a great place to pick up the latest gossip. Both of them were generous with their time and always ready to help. Aliyar was a man of charisma and charm, with some mysterious connections; I've wondered about him all these years. He helped Bert sort out a serious problem at the site and helped a lot of other people too. So I find it shabby that these so-called friends have dropped Hélène now when *they* could be doing something for her. She and Ali lost everything in 1979.'

Ah yes, I thought, the revolution that brought down the monarchy.

She directed me to a small boxy, grey-plastered house in a dip off the main road as she finished telling me this and waved to Hélène, who waited for us in the shade of an untrimmed fig tree. The two women chatted desultorily during the drive to the restaurant, the fields and vineyards soothing to the eye. Our small procession drew a few curious stares as we walked into the restaurant – ash-blond Hélène in a high-necked, hyacinth-blue top and a narrow black skirt, her hair severely drawn back from a fine-boned face. She surveyed the room with cool hazel eyes, gliding on slender shapely legs and stiletto heels next to the smaller Mathilde, voluble, dark-eyed and darker-haired, trailing a brightly coloured silk scarf as she sailed in and took charge. In spite of the Maître d'hôtel's persuasive efforts to place us in the centre of the room, Mathilde insisted on a table by a window, which looked out onto a sunny courtyard with trailing creepers in huge urns and a couple of tables under a lime tree, and generally behaved as if she were the hostess, which did not bother me in the least.

Conversation over lunch was about a much-publicised investigation into the activities of a political figure accused of corruption. Hélène asked me in English, 'You know that saying about pots and kettles. That's what this drama is; not one of that gang is Mr Clean, and they're all making a big noise to divert attention away from themselves.'

When I remarked on the fluency of her English, 'When we lived in Iran it was necessary to speak it for business and on many social occasions. After I left Iran in 1976, I spent some years in the United States in the 1980s.'

'And do you ever go there now?' I asked curiously, wondering whether she visited friends in the large Iranian community there.

She shook her head, and I thought I might have touched upon a delicate subject from the way in which Mathilde veered off on a different tack and asked her in French whether there was any news from a mutual acquaintance.

Towards the end of the meal I mentioned that I was going to stay with friends near Málaga after I left France, at which point I thought a look passed between the two women. They were both in a mellow mood when we left, and I felt it had been a satisfactory afternoon.

Afterwards, when it was just the two of us, 'That was fun, Mathilde. Let's do it again soon; I really enjoyed meeting Hélène. I'm sure she has some interesting stories to tell.'

Little did I know this enthusiasm was going to land me in a difficult situation.

Mathilde rang to thank me again the next morning and asked whether I could stop by to see her later that day.

We sat under a parasol on the terrace, and she started rather hesitantly. 'I know you held down a demanding job and are probably looking forward to doing nothing for a while. I think you'll find, though, that it begins to pall after a while.'

She went on more confidently as I smiled encouragingly, remembering that she had known me when I was a restless, unruly teenager and that there was a good chance that she was right in her assessment. 'You did say that you thought Hélène had some interesting stories to tell. Well, she does, and I wondered whether I could draw you into a project in which I've been engaged.

'I've been recording Hélène's anecdotes and memories, especially the ones of Iran. She knew practically everybody worth knowing, and it seems a shame to lose recollections like hers, which often throw a different light on events than do those of celebrities. I'm hoping there will be enough for eventual publication, if we both last that long. Well, now I find I'm not spending enough time here, and neither she nor I are young enough to put things off. Would you consider taking up where I'm obliged to leave off, ma chérie? It's something dear to my heart, and of course you can stay here as long as you want. I didn't want to bring it up with Hélène until you agreed. If you do, we can work out the details after you've thought about it. I think you should talk to her before making a decision.'

I parried with as many strong reasons against the idea as I could think of on the spur of the moment. 'I'm a translator, not a writer. I'm unfamiliar with the background, the culture and the country. And what makes you think the idea would be acceptable to Hélène?'

'But you *will* be translating; the only difference is that you'll be writing up what's spoken, not already written. And why should she object to your involvement? Both of you got on quite well, didn't you?'

This was going to be tricky. However much I felt like refusing her, I could not dismiss an old family friend who had always been supportive when I had rebelled against my strait-laced parents. I had already had an experience with collaboration, an experiment that had turned sour, and besides, Hélène and I had no history together, no past friendship to encourage her to feel inclined to unburden herself to me. I had, moreover, read enough memoirs by women who had lived in places considered exotic; their various voices, some patronising, some wide-eyed and naive, had made me grind my teeth with irritation. I did not want to be associated with anything of the sort. And yet, there was no graceful way of getting out of it without some show of interest; I did not try very hard to conceal my misgivings from Mathilde as I agreed to take a look at what she already had and then have a chat with Hélène.

I hoped she would consider the role I was to play too intrusive and that I would fail at this last hurdle, but that was not to be; Hélène was perfectly agreeable to the unexpected change of amanuensis in mid-flow, as it were. And flow it was, pouring out like a torrent of which I had to make sense. I was, in fact, to be something more than an amanuensis, I found. I was to shape the whole thing and do the actual writing. *Hoist on my own petard*, I thought. I felt trapped. The apparent freedom to choose had been an illusion; Mathilde was going to have her way.

That afternoon was the beginning of an unusual and unlikely partnership.

***

Hélène's Story
Tehran, 15 July 1956

'Say Balé,' Nasser Ali Pahlavan prompted softly.

'Balé,' I repeated dutifully, eyes lowered in the presence of the mollah.

And so, stifling my giggles at Nasser Ali's irreverently slangy translation of the marriage ceremony, agreeing to heaven knew what, in a language I did not understand, I became the fourth wife of Aliyar Bey Zulgadar. I could hear him in the next room, laughing over a game of cards with a cousin and an old army comrade.

Some weeks earlier, in high spirits and a dusty Citroën with failed brakes, we had arrived in the early hours of the morning at the family mansion in Tehran. The car had brought us from Paris, with a detour to indulge in a short spree on the Côte d'Azur, by way of Rome and Brindisi, Beirut and Baghdad, through miles of desert, and the mountainous regions of western

Iran. Landmines and wars make much of this route hazardous or impracticable today.

The roller-coaster ride with the man who was to mark me for life was to last twenty-five years and began in 1954 in Val-de-Grâce, a military hospital in Paris.

Chapter 2

THE COSSACK'S DAUGHTER

Paris, 1933–43

In the turbulent years following the 1917 Bolshevik Revolution in Russia and the break-up of the tsar's armies, three men – my father, Mikhail Ponomareff, colonel of a Cossack regiment opposing the revolutionary forces; his younger brother, Nikolai, a junior officer in the same regiment, both of them the sons of a privileged family from Rostov-on-Don; and with them, Jascha Artemoff, a soldier who had served under them – made their way to France. Pushed into retreating south towards the Black Sea, the trio then turned west and managed to remain together until they reached the relative safety of France. They were absorbed into that enormous body of displaced people, exiles who came to be known the world over as White Russians, and were usually referred to as *émigrés russes* in France.

The pro-monarchist White armies, which for six years made a stand against the Bolsheviks, the Red armies, had chosen that course of action, but of the millions in that diaspora, many had joined it not for ideological reasons but because they had no choice; like leaves driven by the wind, they fled in any direction that might take them away from the murderous multitudes of marauding peasantry, thus coming to rest in many different lands. A great number came to France, among them my father Mikhail and, quite separately, my mother, Vera Nutsubidze.

In Paris, Mikhail met and fell in love with my mother, a Georgian refugee; I know very little of her life before she met him other than that she had been married to Gregory Khonelidze, her compatriot and the father of my half-sister Lia. Vera, the daughter of landowners, would have found herself destitute had it not been for one accomplishment – the fine embroidery that was taught to all girls of her generation and that had been the pastime of her protected youth. It was to earn her a living in Paris, where fashionable couture houses had plenty of work for her. Papa, like many other Russian émigrés, drove a taxi.

They settled in Clichy, on the north-western limits of the city, a quarter favoured by many others like them. Though separated from her first husband, my mother was still married to him when she met my father and they began their lives together in Paris; economic survival and rebuilding their lives were a priority, and administrative formalities were relegated to a later date – a later date that came when I was already an adult and myself a married woman. When Vera was expecting their child, it was explained to Mikhail that Vera's estranged husband could, if he chose, legally claim her baby as his own, unless that child was born in Mikhail's home. There was no certainty of a divorce being granted before the birth, and my father wanted his child, be it son or daughter, to carry his name without legal tangles over the matter, so I was born in their flat in 1933. They named me Hélène, the French version of Yelyena, my paternal grandmother's name.

My parents retained the formal habits of their earlier lives. Papa, accustomed to being in uniform, would wear a suit to work. Maman worked from home, pursuing her sewing or embroidery quietly in a corner of the living room, as much because it was in her nature to do so as because Papa often worked at night and slept during the earlier part of the day. Not only was our flat small, but women and children, if seen, were not supposed to be heard. Apart from sewing and embroidery, reading was considered a suitable activity for a girl, and I began all three at an early age. There were, in any case, no other children in the household with whom I could play. Lia was already ten years old when I was born and was growing up rebellious and somewhat resentful of me, the new baby.

At home, we spoke Russian, and Papa's lifelong reminder to me was, 'We are Russian, but France gave us refuge, and you were born French.' No identity crisis plagued him, nor were there conflicts in his mind on this subject. His father, Afanasi, who had been chief regional engineer for the imperial railways, had remained in Rostov and survived the massacres and executions of the post-revolution years, probably because he was necessary, in the midst of the power struggles and ever-changing political conditions of the time, to keep a crucial service running. For some years after my father and Uncle Nikolai reached France, they had been able to correspond with their father. Then, in 1927, long before I was born, my grandfather put an end to that by asking them to stop writing. It drew unwelcome attention to the remaining members of the Ponomareff family in Rostov and placed them in danger. With that last link broken, the Russia Papa had left behind disappeared forever; with nothing to go back to, he went forward and taught me much in doing so. The paternal grandmother for whom I had been named had died when my father was quite young, and my meagre knowledge of my Ponomareff grandparents comes from Papa's stories of growing up as the son and eldest child of a wealthy family in Rostov. My inaccessible grandfather's face was known to me from a portrait that hung in our living room; in it, he was portrayed as a sternly expressionless, uniformed, and bemedalled man standing ramrod straight, painted by a man who had never seen him. After settling in Paris, Papa commissioned an artist to paint it from a photograph of his father, which he had managed to keep safe throughout his wanderings. A maxim of my father's, one which has stood me in good stead, was always to buy the best I could afford, as we were not rich enough to buy things that would not last.

My parents did not speak much of their separate and doubtless difficult journeys or how they came to be in France rather than somewhere else. Now that I am an adult and have been close to others who have lived through similar situations, and though this is only conjecture, I believe that they had not chosen to forget, but that more than pride and dignity were involved in their decision not to dwell upon this part of their lives. To speak of the darkness they had seen and lived through themselves would not, in any way, help to secure a happier future for their children or for themselves. We Slavs may be given to introspection, but self-analysis and looking for hidden motivations had not become fashionable and were certainly not a requisite for meaningful conversation. If I cannot now argue with them or their reasoning, I can certainly wish they had not been so reticent on the subject of their earlier lives, for I should have liked to have known more about their youth and about the families I would never have a chance to meet.

In the manner of most exiles, my parents maintained close links with the émigré community, and many of our activities centred on the Russian Orthodox chapel in Clichy. We would meet there for weddings and christenings or for Christmas and Easter Masses, which were heard kneeling or standing up – quite hard on a child and extremely uncomfortable in an unheated church. When I listen to Easter Mass on the radio, a little frisson runs through me, inspired partly by emotion and partly by the memory of the ache in my legs and knees after the time spent on those cold stone floors. Priests are referred to as popes, and a particularity of the Russian Orthodox Church is that there are two categories of clergy, the 'black,' who can marry but remain in the lower ranks, and the 'white,' who remain celibate and can rise to the highest positions. Manya and Yuri Troubnikoff, the children of our pope, were around my age, and I was quite friendly with both of them.

Most émigré children joined the *vityazi*, the scouts, and would also take part in the entertainments organised in the community hall adjacent to the church – concerts, poetry recitals, and plays in Russian. These activities were an invaluable as a way of keeping in touch with the émigré community and also of learning Russian. My generation, whose Russian was acquired in this manner, can be identified by our use of a register and the formal outdated vocabulary and manners of the previous century.

This distinction in our language and behaviour was further reinforced by the fact that the émigré families firmly stayed away from 'the others' (the Soviets). Disdain towards people they considered ignorant boors uncaring of, and unschooled in, the courtesies and manners of a civilised society; outrage that they might be expected to have anything to do with the brutal murderers of their own people; and, additionally, the fear engendered by the potential political dangers of associating with them (a fear which was not unfounded at the time) would all have played a role in a collective decision to keep 'those people' at arm's length. As a result of this, the majority of us, their children, had had no contact with the Soviets until we were adults. I can only infer that our elders discussed all this among themselves, as these were not subjects considered suitable for children. Decades later, I was to find myself living in a house next to the Soviet embassy, with nothing more substantial than a brick wall separating our gardens. I think the proximity bothered its occupants more than it did me.

From the age of three, I used to be sent to spend holidays in the little village of Plazac in the Dordogne. My father's old comrade, Jascha Artemoff, had settled there with his wife, Marfa. They were childless and made a great fuss over me; I called them Tchotcha (aunty) and (Djyadjya) uncle, but they were, in reality, my substitute grandparents. Djyadjya Jascha was now working on a farm attached to the Château de Peuch – one of the many immigrants who fulfilled the urgent need for manpower and farm labour in Europe after the two wars of the twentieth century. These visits continued until I was in my teens, and when I returned to the village some years later to pay my respects at Djyadjya Jascha's grave, I was very moved to find the little farmhouse with the blue shutters exactly as I remembered it.

My first school was the École communale on rue d'Alsace, five minutes from our flat at 16 rue Henri Poincaré. Boys and girls were segregated, and we all wore the standard sleeveless blue tunic of French schoolchildren. The children of the many émigré families living nearby attended the same school, among them the four Poliakoff girls, Olga, Tanya, Militsa, and Marina, whose parents were friendly with mine. All the sisters went on to the ballet school at the opera and later to careers connected with the stage and the cinema. I was closest to Tanya, whose health was delicate, but it was the youngest who, as Marina Vlady, went on to become the best known of the four sisters.

I took piano lessons from an eccentric woman who believed in teaching notes but not scales. When it was time for me to present myself for the entrance exam at the Conservatoire

Rachmaninoff, the examiners had no difficulty in identifying whose pupil I had been when I fumbled my scales. They made due allowance for this, and I got in.

Russian reunions are generally rather jolly affairs, and in our family the most important celebration was on Maman's saint's day, which falls at the end of September. It was unusual in that three saints are honoured together – Vera (truth), for whom my mother was named, Nadyezhda (hope), and Lyubov (love). Guests would start arriving at one o'clock for a meal that lasted through the afternoon. Quantities of vodka and wine would be consumed with the zakuski (starters), usually consisting of pieces of *siliodka*, a kind of salt herring that Russians love; sometimes caviar, or salmon roe, which was my favourite because of its appealing colour. A main course would follow, often the delicate minced veal and chicken patties called *pajarski* or roast pheasant.

In her youth, my mother had never learned how to cook, and it was my father, an accomplished cook, who taught her. She was not much of a drinker either but liked an occasional glass of port or champagne.

No gathering would be complete without a few songs to finish the day, and though Maman had a lovely voice, she could rarely be persuaded to sing. Viktor Omeriki, a Georgian friend, knew how to overcome her shyness. He would begin singing a song and turn to her for 'help' with the words; when she joined in, leaving her glass unattended, Papa would refill it surreptitiously; she would reach for the glass, take a sip, and continue 'helping' Viktor with the words, losing her inhibitions just enough to continue singing through the evening.

Owing to the difference between the Julian and Gregorian calendars, Orthodox Russians observe Christmas a few days later than the Western Church. Papa sometimes worked extra hours over that period, so though they did not throw a party, my parents thought it appropriate to mark those days by giving me a present for each of the two Christmases. This practice might seem overindulgent, but it served to underline what they were trying to teach me – that we were both French and Russian and to affirm and celebrate any one facet of our identities was not a denial of another.

It is Easter – a time of renewal and a resumption of social activity after the winter - that is the most important feast for Orthodox Russians. Easter visits can be made for up to forty days after the Sunday, and for that entire period a 'groaning board' is kept laid to welcome visitors. This custom was all very well in Russia, where a harsh climate and great distances could make social visits strenuous, but it was hardly needed as we crisscrossed the quartier to call on all the émigré families within reach. We would all exchange the traditional greeting 'Christos vosskresse' (Christ is risen) as we came in and were offered kulitch and paskha. Over the Easter weekend, the men would make their rounds on one day, and the women on the next. The days before Easter were taken up in preparing *kulitch* and paskha[1], which symbolised the laden table. These were offered to everybody who looked in, and there was, of course, much toasting and knocking back of vodka and other spirits.

One year, my father decided that I could accompany him as a substitute for the son he did not have. So many of the men had been in the army that, in private, they often addressed each other by their old military ranks. Thinking back on that now, I see that perhaps they all behaved as if they might yet be called upon to return to arms, as if the monarchy could be restored and they could take up their old lives. But I wonder how many truly believed it could actually happen so many years later. They thought it reprehensible that the tsar and his family had not been saved by his cousin, the king of England. All it needed, they agreed, was to send his yacht to rescue them – an easy matter for one who had a whole navy at his disposal. They themselves had their lives but had lost their whole world, sometimes their entire families, and a way of life that, in their different ways, they had all fought courageously and hard to save. It would be churlish to begrudge them the harmless nostalgia that gave them a sense of identity and belonging, which allowed them, the survivors, to keep alive the memory of what would never be seen again. While they chatted in low voices about old campaigns and General Wrangel[2], tiny glasses of something sweet would be brought out for me at every stop we made; several visits and several glasses

---

[1] *Kulitch* resembles cheesecake, and paskha is like the Italian panettone. Both are traditional Russian Easter sweets.

[2] General Wrangel, with General Denikin, led the White Armies opposing the Bolsheviks; he and his forces were eventually evacuated from the Crimea.

The Fourth Wife of Aliyar Bey

later, I felt quite sick – I had to be carried home up three flights and experienced my first hangover the next day. I think that was in 1938, after I had just turned five.

I was a little over six at the beginning of the war in 1939, and though I could barely understand what it would mean for us, I remember the Germans occupying Paris in 1940. After this, Papa was attached to the staff of a German admiral as his personal chauffeur and was away quite a lot. The two of them used to spend their time between Paris and the coast in and around Boulogne-sur-mer. Papa used to wear the Russian eagle pinned to the underside of his collar, and when he wanted to go into a restaurant or café where he would not normally have been allowed, he would flash it quickly at the guards, who naturally thought it was a German eagle and that he was an officer who had a reason not to flaunt his status. Very likely he did the same in other, more dangerous situations, as he was using his position, and the admiral's car, to help the Resistance. It is also likely that the admiral was aware of this and not disapproving, as he would often say to Papa, 'You are off duty for the evening, Mikhail; take the car if you wish.'

Once, when he and Papa were in Paris, the admiral invited us to have tea at La Madeleine, a smart café that was a great favourite among German officers. The occasion was memorable for two reasons: I had an ice cream, a rare treat at any time and more so in wartime Paris, and I was given a present that became my most cherished possession. After tea, the admiral invited us to stroll with him as he browsed through the wares of the second-hand bookstalls that line the quais along the Seine. I stopped to admire a collection of Mozart pieces bound in red leather, which the admiral promptly bought for me. I refused to leave it behind when, like other children of my age, I was evacuated out of Paris and sent to the safety of the countryside.

Children who had no family outside the city were sent to complete strangers, and it was my good luck to be able to go to Djyadjya Jascha and Tchotcha Marfa, who received me with open arms. Some of my contemporaries spent the period of their evacuation in relative luxury but may not have felt the sense of security I did with the Artemoffs. Whatever the conditions in which we spent those years, those of us who were children at that time know that we owe a debt of gratitude to the generosity of the many who took us in and kept us as safe as they could.

I was in Plazac for a little over a year and did not feel at all deprived in all that time. I adjusted quickly to wearing wooden clogs and walking one and a half kilometres to school; I learnt to speak the patois and how to keep a watchful eye on the grazing cows; a neighbour taught me how to spin as we sat tending her flock of sheep, and I soon had enough rough wool to knit myself two pairs of the thick socks we wore under our clogs. Except for a Russian-style oven, constructed in collaboration with the local blacksmith, the farmhouse was no different from those around us, with a main room, quite literally a living room, and a sleeping chamber, which had three beds piled high with blankets and quilts, each in its own corner. Built in the local pale golden stone, it had plastered whitewashed walls and blue wooden shutters.

The unoccupied château belonged in a fairy tale, rising tall on an outcrop of rock, set in the varying greens of the surrounding fields and the woods farther away. Stone outhouses were dotted about its extensive grounds; the mill house was occupied by a young couple, Christiane and her husband, Louis, the nephew of the owners, the Barbets. Tchotcha Marfa used to take me with her into the big house and allow me to wander about the rooms as she swept and dusted. Of its many rooms, my favourite was the music room with the piano, at which I practised whenever I could. It occurs to me now to wonder how it was kept tuned.

'Monsieur Jacques' as Djyadjya Jascha was called in the village, was known to like his drink, and he would say, 'So shall we go and have some cherries, sweetheart?'

The two of us would take a small glass and a spoon out to the barn, where there was a shelf with a row of bottles containing cherries harvested from the tree outside the cottage and preserved in alcohol. He would spoon out a couple of cherries, pour a shot of the fruit-infused alcohol over them, and down it in a gulp, leaving the two liqueur-soaked cherries at the bottom of the glass for me. If Tchotcha Marfa objected, as she often did, his excuse was that he was giving me a much-deserved treat for being such a good child. At other times, we would trudge up to the village bar halfway up the hill, where he would enjoy a gossip over a glass of red wine and occasionally something stronger; I would sometimes be given a sip before being sent to play in the shade of the trees outside. It is a wonder that I am not an alcoholic today.

Chapter 3

A Joyless Marriage

Paris 1943–51

Paris was still an occupied city when I returned from Plazac. Lia had begun to spend a lot of time at home with two old schoolmates, Pierre and Etienne Lacroix. Their father, Admiral Lacroix, was the man responsible for issuing orders to scuttle the French fleet in order to prevent it from falling into German hands. They would often bring along Willi, a young German whom they had known in peacetime. It was a friendship that might not have existed if Willi had been of a different temperament. He had been a student at the Conservatoire in Paris when war was declared, and he could not have avoided reporting for service when he was called up by his government. Nor, as a German national, could he have remained at large in France, where he would have been declared a deserter by the Germans and targeted as fair game by the French.

My parents had no reason to object to his presence, for they realised he was a peaceful young man who had no control over a situation that made him as unhappy as it did us. He was sensitive enough to wear civilian dress rather than his uniform when he visited us and behaved towards everybody with a gentle old-fashioned courtesy. As he was also a fine pianist, it was not long before we became fond of him and looked forward to his visits. We had news of him many years after the war was over and were relieved to discover that he had lived through it and been able to complete his musical studies. He had become a teacher of music and a father of nine – perhaps he was trying to follow in the footsteps of the Bachs, father and son, whose music he greatly admired.

Papa's old boss, the admiral, appears to have been less fortunate, for we could find no trace of him when we made enquiries after the war. We wanted to thank him for saving Papa's life and to let him know that Papa had come through the war safely. It was towards the end of the war that the admiral had said, 'Mikhail, we have a problem; you'd better disappear.' And Papa left immediately to go into hiding. For a year, Maman and I had no idea whether he was dead or alive, in a prison camp or at liberty, but whatever it was that he did during that time merited a certificate in recognition of his services to his adopted country.

By this time, I was old enough to attend the Lycée Jules Ferry on the Place Clichy. The school was not far from the metro station, which doubled as a public shelter during bomb alerts. We would all rush there when the sirens sounded. Even though it was only three stops away from home on the metro, Maman decided, quite illogically, that I would be safer travelling to school in a first-class compartment. On one occasion, when I was the only passenger in the compartment, a German officer came in with a young woman. They made for the seats opposite me, and he ordered me out, with arm outstretched and finger pointing towards the exit, loudly shouting, 'Raus.' It made me so furious that, instead of going to another compartment, I got off the train and caught the next one. This was not one of the days on which I wore my favourite pleated skirt, which, with wartime shortages, was made of paper. I would iron it carefully before putting it on and refuse to sit down until I got to school, in order to arrive in class looking neat and uncrushed.

When the war ended, I wanted to visit Djyadjya Jascha and Tchotcha Marfa in Plazac. I had done the journey so often that my parents felt I would be fine by myself once they put me on the train. I was so excited at the thought of being back in Plazac, I jumped off one station early. The stationmaster came across when he saw me looking around the unfamiliar station. There would be no train until the next day, so he took me home to his wife. I spent the night in their spare bedroom, and he put me on the train the following day, with instructions to the conductor to make sure I got off at the next station. I waited at the bus stop just outside the station for the bus, which would normally have dropped me within sight of the farm, until the stationmaster came out to ask me what I was doing there.

'I am going to M Artemoff's,' I said.

'Ah, to Monsieur Jacques! But, ma petite, have you forgotten that the bus doesn't run on Sundays?'

Undaunted, I pulled some night things and a toothbrush from my case, stuffed them into my satchel, and slung it over my shoulder with my newly acquired roller skates. The station's master watched my preparations with a bemused air and agreed to send my suitcase to Plazac on the bus the following day. The road climbs from the station, and I passed the bus driver's house as I trudged up the hill. He too came out, wanting to know where I was going. I explained once again that I was going to stay with my uncle, M Artemoff. He apologised for not being able to run the bus for a single passenger, but he and his wife gave me lunch and sent me on my way. I continued towards the top of the hill, from where I planned to skate down a curving road, starting at Rouffignac, down through the village of Plazac, into the small valley where the Château de Peuch and its farmhouse are located. It was a six-kilometre run on a road that I am unlikely to forget and an exploit that went into the annals of village lore.

At the top of the hill, I stared in confused incomprehension at the burnt and blackened wrecks of the buildings of a village that could be not be anything but Rouffignac.[3] I knew nothing of this particular tragedy but had seen enough destruction to waste no time in confounded speculation. I put on my skates and pushed off with great confidence. I had overlooked the fact that I had no means of controlling my speed, and I realised that only after I was already on my way down. I went hurtling past

---

[3] The Germans burnt Rouffignac on 31 March 1944; the church and the bakery remained standing, and the present village was reconstructed after 1945. The baker pointed out to the Germans that, if they burnt down his establishment, they would have no bread.

startled peasants out in the fields and, further on, a group of old men sitting over their drinks at tables outside the bar in Plazac. Speed and apprehension had made me breathless as I coasted to a stop where the road levelled out next to the farm. I undid my skates and went looking for Tchotcha Marfa and Djyadjya Jascha. He was teased for the rest of his life about his little niece who had flashed through the village like an arrow.

When I revisited the area almost sixty years after that holiday, I found the château is now screened from the road by the trees over which it once towered. Fashions have changed, and plastered walls are no longer the norm. The white plaster has been scraped off the walls of the farmhouse to expose the stone underneath. I remember now with great regret something Papa told us just after the war. He had heard from Djyadjya Jascha that the château was up for sale at a reasonable price because the owner wanted to be rid of it. He considered buying it but had to drop the idea as the place was in such a state of disrepair after years of neglect that it would have cost more than he could raise to put it in order. The Château de Peuch has remained one of the most dominant landmarks in the magical landscape of the memories of my childhood.

***

Papa was back in Paris but would not speak of his year in hiding. He went back to the old routine at his usual stand on the Place Pigalle, often passing by Les Halles to pick up some fresh produce before returning home to cook himself a meal in the early hours of the morning. Most mornings, I would wake up to an appetising smell and share a bit of his dinner for breakfast before leaving for school. Maman was still executing sewing and embroidery commissions, and Lia was working as a secretary at Maison Karyinska in rue Washington, a street better known for its nocturnal traffic than for its more mundane daytime occupations – well-dressed prostitutes came out after dark, and plush cars cruised past in the evenings. Maison Karyinska specialised in costumes for the theatre and the ballet and was closely associated with the costume and set designer Andrei Vakyévitch.

I was sent to the Collège Fénélon in Cambrai, north of Paris, where I was to spend the following three years. Lia's wild behaviour had begun to worry my parents, and they thought that a strict boarding school for girls, away from the temptations of Paris, might delay, if not prevent, me from trying to emulate her. The principal of the school, whom we all addressed as Mademoiselle, had instructions not to allow me out under any circumstances.

Most students went home for the weekend, and those three years might have been a lonely time had it not been for Nicole Douzedamme, a classmate whose family had a comfortable house in the town. When I was invited to spend a weekend with them, Mademoiselle sensibly decided that ignoring my parents' instructions was better than having me mope about miserably every weekend; I was sent off with cautions that it was to remain our secret. I ended up spending every other weekend with the Douzedamme family. I kept my word to Mademoiselle and only told my parents of it when, many years later, I told them how Nicole Douzedamme and I found ourselves living in Iran and had met again.

I was sixteen in 1949 when my parents brought me back to live at home. Paris was returning to a semblance of normality. Maman was busier than ever with commissions for fine embroidery from the couture houses, and I was allowed to earn some pocket money by modelling for them if they needed a replacement or an extra body. As Girl Friday at Karyinska's, my sister Lia was tasked with finding the fabrics required for making up the costumes after Andrei Vakyévitch had finalised them with the client.

Not long after this, Vakyévitch began designing theatre and film sets and often worked with Jean-Louis Barrault and Madeleine Renaud's theatre company. Rationing and shortages had made the sourcing of fabrics a task worthy of a detective and Lia would take me along as her helper on this treasure hunt. We would chase all over Paris, rummage in suppliers' storerooms, and pounce triumphantly on the few lengths of silks and velvets, trimmings and fripperies that had been carefully hidden away during the war and had survived it.

Marina Fyodorovna, Karyinska's chief seamstress, did not like using the wooden dummies used as a template. She often used me as a live one, particularly when she was making something for Edwige Feuillère[4], whose waist measurements were the same as

---

[4] Edwige Feuillère was a stage and screen star.

mine. Occasionally, I would also be called to try on costumes for the dancers of the Marquis de Cuevas ballet company.

A perquisite of Lia's job was that she could invite me to dress rehearsals, which were held in the Théâtre Marigny on the Champs-Elysées; I was, thus, able to see many plays and ballets for which I could not have afforded tickets. If I was out late, I would stop by the taxi stand in Place Pigalle, hoping to find Papa free to give me a ride home. When he was not there, his friend General Zouboff would run me back in his taxi, and if I had the bad manners to offer to pay, he would tap his cheek for a kiss in payment and send me in with admonitions to go straight upstairs to Maman.

Tanya Poliakoff was not in good health and had been sent to regain her strength in Versoix, a village near Geneva. She chose 'Odile Versois' as her stage name. She had turned eighteen and had just made her first film *Dernières Vacances*. She invited a small group of girlfriends to see it. I remember the occasion chiefly because Tanya had admitted to us that she was very embarrassed by a scene in which a young admirer lovingly refers to her 'beautiful hands,' which she thought were her worst feature. She said she hoped nobody would actually look at them on the screen. It was enough to provoke us into making perfect nuisances of ourselves, nudging each other and giggling as we made loud remarks about her 'beautiful hands'.

The war had ended just as my friends and I had reached the age when young people begin thinking of their futures. Ali Kobakhidze wanted to be an architect, and his younger

The Fourth Wife of Aliyar Bey

brother, Georges, planned to become a dentist; both of them were wonderful dancers and earned money to pay for their studies by performing in Russian nightclubs. Yuri Troubnikoff planned to become an engineer; his sister, Manya, hoped to marry a Frenchman with whom she had fallen in love, though it was definitely not the thing done in my parents' circle. We were expected to marry people of a similar ethnic and cultural background. Manya had made me swear not to tell Lia until she herself was ready to speak to her parents, as Lia could be quite snobbish about such things and was also a bit of a mischief-maker. Manya's parents might have felt humiliated and reacted angrily if they had heard about this from somebody other than Manya herself. I was pleased when Manya married her Frenchman, to whom she remains happily married to this day. My own ambition was to study law.

The war years had affected my health, and during my last year at school I had to stay home for some months. In the optimism of that post-war period and the enthusiasm of youth, I thought of it as a short delay before I took my final school-leaving exams and went to university. In the meanwhile, and also looking to the future, my parents announced my engagement to Alexander Elrikh, a young man of Russo-German parentage.

In another time and another place, before they all came to France, Elrikh's Siberian mother, Taïssia, had formed a close friendship with Maman. For reasons which were never made clear to me, Taïssia committed suicide when her son was ten years old. Traumatised by this loss, the boy looked to my mother, *his* mother's dearest friend, for comfort and began calling her Maman; she, in turn, became very protective of him. Our marriage was the result of that old friendship between our mothers and Maman's belief that she was responsible for her dead friend's son. She wanted to bring him into the family, and Elrikh himself desired and sought the match; I was given no choice in the matter. My upbringing made it unthinkable to disobey my parents on a matter as serious as this, and I could not think of any viable alternatives.

At the time of our engagement, Elrikh was a cadet at St Cyr[5]. That is probably why Papa raised no objection when Maman put forward the proposal, nor, knowing what he surely knew about the young man's family and the reasons for Taïssia's suicide, did he look closely into the character of the man I was to marry.

I had known Elrikh all my life, and did not like him. Though I knew it was no more than a postponement of the inevitable, with the cooperation of my friends, I was able to make sure that I was never left alone with him.

Our engagement and my obvious dislike of him did not prevent him from leaving me to deal with the attempted suicide of his mistress during a cadets' party in a friend's flat. An ambulance was called, and while everybody waited for it, Elrikh left me alone in a room with her, keeping watch as she lay, half-conscious, on a divan. Nobody else I knew behaved like

---

[5] St Cyr was one of the two most prestigious military academies in France.

Elrikh or his mistress, and inexperienced as I was in the ways of the world, I did not know whether I would be held directly or indirectly responsible for this or for whatever happened next. I was in a state of uncomprehending alarm and shock, though I managed to look calm. It may have been an attempt on Elrikh's part to make me grow up, but it only served to reinforce the distaste I felt for him. In the tight-lipped solidarity of youth, none of my friends mentioned the incident to their parents or mine. I saw no way out, unless I cared to inform them myself of this unpleasant incident. And to my later regret, embarrassment and timidity won the day.

In August 1951, six months after my eighteenth birthday, my parents and their friends gathered around us in the Russian chapel in rue Montevidéo to celebrate my marriage to a man who frightened and revolted me.

Chapter 4

ALGERIA

1952-1954

After Elrikh graduated with honours from St Cyr, he was eligible for the Foreign Legion which could take its pick from the best. He spent a year training at the officers' school in St Maixent, while I became pregnant. He travelled to Algeria to join his new regiment late in summer 1952, just after the birth of our daughter, whom we had named Taïssia after her paternal grandmother. My baby daughter and I joined him when she was barely two months old, and I settled into the legion's compound in Maskara, with Willi, our enormous German batman, to help me.

Whether it was to test the mettle of Lieutenant Elrikh's young wife or the authenticity of my Cossack blood, my first visit to the mess turned out to be something of a challenge for which nobody had prepared me. It could have been because such a thing had never occurred before; women were not expected to be able to drink like troopers – well, not the officers' wives, at any rate. I stared uncertainly at a tumbler containing a gaudy-looking concoction of red and green, which are the colours of the legion. This was supposed to be drunk in a single shot. Half a glassful of rough red wine floated on a thick foundation of crème de menthe. Needless to say it was quite vile, but I managed to throw it back, gagging and coming up for air but pleased with myself for having met the challenge and for not having let our side down – not only my father and Uncle Nikolai, but all the Russians and Georgians who were well-represented in the legion in the twentieth century.

In the 1st REC, a cavalry regiment, a squadron leader once counted 128 Russians in his 156-strong force, among them Cossacks, regular cavalrymen and ex-officers, including an erstwhile general and a colonel. The break-up of the tsar's Imperial Guard and the royalist regiments, known as the White Army, had dispersed the Russians. The Georgians had been driven into exile by the Bolshevik absorption of their homeland. Their training had been rigorous and traditional; all had seen active service. And painfully short of skills and manpower, depleted by the Great War of 1914–18, the armies of Western Europe welcomed them. Many officers became instructors in military academies. This was the case in France, where they taught at both St Cyr and St Maixent[6]; the enlisted men went wherever they could.

The Foreign Legion was also a logical choice for the many who had been officers but were now unable to find a suitable military opening. Having no wish to try to adjust to civilian

---

[6] St Cyr was the academy for cadets, St Maixent for officers.

life, they preferred life in the ranks.[7] When it came to cavalry regiments, both groups had an obvious edge over most other applicants – their horsemanship. I have often wondered why Papa made the choice he did. Why drive a car in Paris when he could have led a life that more closely resembled the one he had left? He claimed it was because he did not want to go away after he met Maman.

Horsemanship was, of course, irrelevant in Elrikh's case, as he had joined the 1st REI, an infantry regiment. While I settled down to life as a housewife and mother, Elrikh was caught up in patrols, exercises, and whatever else his work entailed. Any spare time he had was spent with his cameras or in the darkroom he'd set up in our flat. Photography was, for him, more than a hobby, and he pursued it with a Teutonic determination and disregard for all else. He was not of a sociable nature, and if his comrades stopped by to invite us to join them for a film or to go on some other excursion, he would emerge from the darkroom for long enough to refuse but would suggest that they take me along. It was clear for all to see that I was being sent off in much the same manner as one does an irritating child.

***

Not long after my arrival, while I was still settling in, Tanya Poliakoff spent a night with us in what turned out to be a memorable visit for the whole mess. She also left behind an

---

[7] While inspecting the line-up of applicants, the duty colonel once asked a small-built man, no longer young, his profession before applying to join the legion. 'I was a general, colonel, sir.'

The Fourth Wife of Aliyar Bey

unusual reminder of her stay. Tanya had already made several films, but on this visit to North Africa, she was on a theatre tour. When I mentioned her by her stage name, Odile Versois, noting she had been a childhood friend and was coming on a flying visit, the junior officers expressed their eagerness to meet her and began arranging a lunch in her honour. She accepted our invitation to come and stay for a night between performances and attend the lunch.

We set off to fetch her in a borrowed car, and it was midnight by the time we returned with her. We had promised to look in at the mess before going up to our flat, and we went in expecting one or two night owls to be about. It seemed that the entire complement of junior officers was waiting up for us, and they all stood up politely when we came in. Tanya broke the ice by announcing that she was starving and would somebody take her to the kitchen to get some bread and cheese. It became very merry after that.

During lunch the next day, some of the senior officers and their wives 'just looked in to say hallo, unable to believe reports that the junior officers were playing host to such a popular actress. As some of them had been sceptical of my knowing anybody worth meeting, I felt rather satisfied at having proven them wrong.

Tanya was appearing on stage in Oran that evening, and while we were driving her to the theatre, she insisted we stop at a bathroom supplies shop. We were unfamiliar with the city and ended up at an extremely expensive showroom in a smart area, where she bought a mahogany toilet seat. This she signed with a flourish and presented to me, to add a luxurious touch to my otherwise rather Spartan bathroom. Word got around, and our visitors would often make some excuse to go into the bathroom just to inspect it.

***

In early 1953, when Elrikh's regiment received orders to leave for Indochina[8], I made plans to return to Paris. It was an opportunity, I thought, to reclaim my life, to explain the situation to my parents, and to start afresh. I gave Elrikh no inkling of my intentions; all I told him was that I might as well return to Paris while he was away. He forbade it, on the grounds that I was now an officer's wife and my place was not with what he contemptuously called 'that pathetic bunch of exiled has-beens'. It was high time, he told me, that I grew up and learnt that life was for living, not for nostalgia. Furious and disappointed, I remained in Maskara, and consoled myself with the knowledge that he would be far away and was unlikely to return very soon.

Eager though I had been to return to Paris, staying on in Maskara allowed me a freedom I had never known when I was still unmarried and living with my parents or, until now, as Mrs Alexander Elrikh. In the months that followed Elrikh's departure, I did indeed grow up and start living fully; I began enjoying myself and fell in love.

---

[8] Vietnam, Laos, and Cambodia made up the former French Indochina.

The Fourth Wife of Aliyar Bey

With Elrikh gone, I no longer had the right to a batman, so there was no Willi to help out during the week. He missed Taïssia, whom he always addressed as Poopsie, his diminutive for *poupée*[9], and would come to see us every Sunday, his day off. He would spend the day fussing over her; he would play with her, bathe her, and lovingly iron every tiny pleat in her smocked dresses while she had her nap.

Elrikh's absence on active duty carried a material advantage in the form of an extra family allowance, so I felt I could afford a prolonged holiday. The need to escape the torrid summer heat of North Africa gave me an excuse to go to France. I let it be thought that I was taking Taïssia to visit Elrikh's father and stepmother on their poultry farm near Mougins, but I had absolutely no intention of being stuck for several weeks with my uninteresting parents-in-law and their smelly clucking chickens. Instead, I rented an apartment in Cannes for three months.

***

Taïssia and I used to spend our days at the beach, where we made the acquaintance of an extremely sympathetic American naval officer whose ship was in port for the US Navy's annual goodwill visit. The man watched Taïssia, a chubby blond baby playing happily in the sand, for a while with a wide smile on his face and then walked over and requested my permission to join us. He said he missed his family and began spending his free mornings or afternoons on the beach playing with Taïssia.

---

[9] A doll

Those hours helped to improve my English, and making adult conversation made a refreshing change. I was invited to dinner on his ship, the *Coral Sea*, and remember the occasion mostly for the stark contrast between the sumptuousness of the meal and the appointments on the ship and the shortages of which we were not entirely free in post-war Europe. I had had no reason to feel deprived after the war was over. In the Foreign Legion, we were very well provided for, but there was a luxury and abundance in evidence on the *Coral Sea* that was still missing on our side of the Atlantic.

Taïssia had her first birthday that August, and then it was time for us to go back.

***

The end of each summer brought fresh arrivals from France, and that year's intake was already installed when I returned to Algeria in September. Among them were Jean and Marie Seitz, Cocotte and George Maroni, Lieutenant Peigné, and the rather jolly Captain Potus. Lastly there was André Montagné, who became my lover and was my first love.

The war in Indochina was not going well, and the mood on the compound was quite glum. The commanding officer decided that the arrival of these new officers would provide an excuse to arrange a special occasion to cheer us all up. He threw a dinner party in the mess, to which he invited the junior officers who were not on patrol or on a posting and all the wives, even those whose husbands were away. We were seated at a long table, and halfway through the meal, with Jean Seitz on my right and André on my left, I felt a gentle pressure against my left foot. I found my neighbour rather attractive, but felt it was too public an occasion and improper for me as a married woman to encourage him. I leant towards Jean on my right and whispered an embarrassed request for advice on how to deal with it; he suggested I allow it to continue until he nudged me. I interpreted this as dispensation to flirt and responded confidently, withdrawing my foot when Jean gave me the signal. He stretched out his foot to take over and it was quite a while before André discovered that he had been playing footsie with Jean.

André was twenty-four and a bachelor. I was twenty and felt I owed no loyalty to an absent husband who had shown little interest in me other than as a possession. Neither of us kept office hours, and we lived on the same compound. The inevitable affair began without soul-searching or logistical problems. We were careful and discreet, and I was too young to know that it would not suffice; it was just as inevitable that the commanding officer would come to know of our liaison; I received a summons from Colonel Jean-Pierre.

The colonel's benign and cheerful manner had earned him his nickname, Soleil. I did not expect that sunny nature to be in evidence when I arrived at his office, convinced that André's career would suffer and that I would be blamed for it. The colonel was a father figure to all of us, and though there was little he could do to me, other than express disapproval, I felt ashamed and nervous before him.

'My child, we are all aware of how unhappy you were with your husband, and I cannot blame you for what is happening just now. I do ask you, however, that you be discreet and not get yourself talked about. My wife agrees with me that, as long as both of you conduct yourselves sensibly, we will all turn a blind eye to it and nothing further will be said.'

If he spoke to André in sterner terms, I never learned of it.

Those were blissful months. André and I continued our affair with due regard for the colonel's warning but with no other constraints upon us.

On New Year's Day of 1954, the senior officers threw their usual party for us in their mess, and on 6 January, the junior officers reciprocated. Our celebration that year was enlivened by an enterprising sergeant who had ferreted out a Russian legionnaire with an accordion. The man did not need much persuasion to come and play for us, or rather, for the free drinks that had been promised. It turned out to be a very Slavic evening, and with the music getting wilder as the evening progressed, I was unable to hold myself back. I kicked off my shoes; was hoisted onto the bar by Jean Seitz; pulled the musician along; and, petticoats swirling, proceeded to dance an energetic

The Fourth Wife of Aliyar Bey

Kassachuk[10] with him. It must have been the luck of the very drunk that kept us both from falling off the narrow bar counter.

A growing popular movement for Algerian independence kept the legion and other French troops posted in the country busily occupied. Neither did it look as though the insurgency in Indochina was going to be suppressed easily or quickly, so it was clear to those of us who were in Algeria that it could not be long before more troops would be have to be diverted from the Algerian trouble to fight in Indochina.

In May 1954, inconceivable as it was to us, the French Army lost a decisive battle at Dien Bien Phu to Vietnamese forces commanded by General Giap. The first I knew of it was when some of the officers and their wives came hammering on my door late at night. At twenty-one, I was by far the youngest wife there, and they felt I ought not be left alone. A further incentive for them to wake me up was that, as a result of Elrikh's passion for gadgets and all things mechanical, we had the most powerful radio in the junior officers' quarters.

A group of us crowded around it, horror-stricken and unable to believe the reports of rout and disarray, carnage and retreat. Whatever my feelings towards Elrikh, this was most certainly not how I wanted our marriage to end. I was worried for him and, indeed, for all our men there.

---

[10] A Ukrainian dance with an increasing tempo in which the woman leads and indicates movement changes with handclaps

Later, I learnt that he was part of the company that had endeavoured to force a passage through surrounding enemy troops while protecting their comrades.[11]

André received the expected orders to leave for Indochina. We had decided to get married when he returned. Without mentioning André, I had already written to Elrikh to inform him that I wished to end our marriage, so there was no further reason for me to remain in Algeria. I planned to begin divorce proceedings in Paris while André was away; I dared not entertain the possibility that he might not return. He went off to Indochina, and blithely, I prepared to go home to my parents and wait for my man to come back.

I expected to return to Maskara as André's wife, so I did not believe this was a good-bye to the legion or to Algeria. I was walking away from an unpleasant period in my life, and I experienced a heady sense of power in being able to do so.

The battle of Dien Bien Phu was the turning point for France, though its withdrawal from Indochina was not the end of that particular war. The growing movement for Algerian independence took heart from this French defeat and escalated its activity. It was to be a further eight years, marked by bloody conflicts, before Algeria gained its independence in 1962. The Foreign Legion was obliged to transfer its headquarters from Sidi-bel-Abbès to Aubagne, near Marseilles.

---

[11] Colonne crève-coeur

Georges Maroni died in Indochina. His wife, Cocotte, reading her tarot cards one night, knew she had been widowed before she was officially notified the next day. Colonel Jean-Pierre, dear 'Soleil', to whom I am still grateful for his understanding and kindness, died in Algeria in a helicopter accident. Yet others whom we had known became embroiled in the confrontation between General de Gaulle and the mutinous factions of French armed forces. Unwelcome in France and unable to remain in Algeria, many who had taken part in these abortive attempts to keep Algeria French went to live in countries where their participation in these events was either not known or did not matter.

Chapter 5

THE FORMATION OF THE FRENCH FOREIGN LEGION

In 1831 a royal ordinance was approved by the Chamber of Deputies in Paris. It authorised the formation of a new corps to be called the Foreign Legion. It could not be based in France, and, as the name indicates, it was to be composed solely of foreigners. France's relatively small army was made up mainly of young and untrained conscripts serving their time. Diminishing public appetite for France's adventures abroad made it difficult to attract recruits, and the new legion would serve a dual purpose – troops would be available for foreign campaigns, and there would be less political pressure and public outcry if they were not French citizens.

Foreigners in the service of a country that was not their own were no novelty. Public opinion of the time had begun to incline towards national armies and against the presence of mercenaries, who were increasingly viewed as unreliable and expensive. To counter this, it was argued that the structure of the new force would be quite different from the earlier practice of retaining full companies with their own officers, answering to their own captains. The new legion would be composed of troops who could not be regarded as mercenaries because they would be recruited as individuals and placed under the direct command of French officers. This rule regarding the nationality of officers remains in force; commanding officers are French, and it is unusual for foreigners to be promoted to senior ranks in the legion.

The most convincing argument in favour of establishing this new fighting force was one that was not spelt out. Since its own revolution in 1789, France had become a haven for political dissidents and revolutionaries; political upheavals during and immediately after the Napoleonic era had wrought social and demographic changes all over Europe. In France, the influx of foreigners had grown to unmanageable proportions in that first quarter of the nineteenth century, and many who could not find work had taken to banditry.

If a further deterioration in law and order was to be forestalled, some way of absorbing these immigrants had to be found. Here, then, was a solution that would remove from mainland France a lot of unruly elements that could not be integrated into the fabric of daily life and give them an opportunity to serve the country that had received them. Whatever their reasons for having left their own countries, they were being offered a job with pay, with the promise of anonymity and French citizenship at the end of a five-year contract. In the meantime, there would be soldiering and adventure enough to keep them occupied somewhere far away. Many had nowhere else to go.

Late in the 19th century the Legion established its headquarters at Sidi-bel-Abbès in Algeria. Throughout the 20th century, the Foreign Legion was so strongly associated with North Africa, and, in the second half of the century for its role in French Indochina, that its participation in other campaigns has been largely overlooked. In the first twenty-five years of its existence, it had been sent not only to Algeria but also to Spain and Crimea.[12] These early campaigns served to vindicate its creation and its first supporters by establishing the effectiveness of the legion, but it was only in Mexico, after the battle of Camerone in 1863 that it won recognition and respect; on its return to France it was decorated for exceptional bravery in the face of overwhelming odds.

In 1861, influential European investors who had suffered substantial losses in Mexico brought pressure to bear upon their governments to obtain their help to recover the money. France and Spain, along with Britain, sent troops to Mexico. This joint expedition met with very little success, and Spain and Britain recalled their troops in 1862. Napoleon III, whose ambitions went beyond the original goal of recouping the investors' losses, expected that a better-equipped and better-trained army was capable of overcoming any opposition the Mexicans might

---

[12] Lord Raglan, the commander of the Anglo-French alliance during the Crimean War, kept on forgetting that the Napoleonic wars were over and that the French were now allies and not enemies. He kept on referring to the enemy (the Russians) as 'the French'.

put up, and French troops were ordered to stay on and occupy the country. To the general surprise of all, the population turned out to be anything but meek and the French met with unexpectedly stalwart resistance from the Mexicans. Illness and disease further slowed the progress of the campaign. Two companies from the legion were dispatched from North Africa as reinforcements for the regulars.

In 1863, one of these two companies left the coastal town of Vera Cruz on a sortie to the interior and was surrounded by Mexican troops in the village of Camerone. Disdainful of his enemy's military ability, bravery, and equipment, the company's commanding officer, Captain Danjou, refused the Mexicans' offer of an honourable surrender. Exacting from his men a vow to fight to the death, he fell early in the battle. But the legionnaires fought through the day, inflicting heavy casualties on the Mexicans. The last three legionnaires left standing were once more invited by the Mexicans to surrender. This they did, and they and their wounded comrades were eventually returned to their own side as part of an exchange of prisoners.

The men of the legion had gained the admiration and respect of the Mexicans, but the campaign itself was proving as unpopular in France as the presence of its troops was in Mexico. It was a protracted and costly war; apart from sickness among the men and a significant number of desertions that had begun to deplete the ranks, there was very little to show after six years of fighting. The French government recalled its demoralised troops in 1867. Though the Mexican adventure had not been a success for France, the legion came out of it covered in glory and was awarded the *Légion d'Honneur* for its stand at Camerone. It was the beginning of its reputation for ferocity, for solidarity and loyalty to comrades-in-arms, and for its willingness to fight under any and all conditions. But it was still not welcome to remain on French soil.

The disparate men who formed the legion had no common country, language, or culture, no natural ties which drew them together or called them back to wherever they had once called home. The authorities felt that something more tangible than the legion's motto 'Legio Patria Nostra'[13] was needed, and it was agreed that a home base would give the legion a sense of permanence and an appearance of respectability. The choice fell upon the little town of Sidi-bel-Abbès in Algeria, a short distance from the Mediterranean coast and accessible enough from mainland France.

With nothing to bind to one another these rootless and homeless men, whose reasons for joining the legion were as varied as they themselves – they had shed old loyalties and past history – esprit de corps would have to be inspired and instilled by drawing upon the shared experiences of the men. The battle of Camerone had been, up to that time, the legion's most glorious hour, and 30 April, the day on which it took place, was chosen as the legion's commemorative day.

---

[13] The Legion is our Fatherland.

The Fourth Wife of Aliyar Bey

Captain Danjou, hero of that battle, had left behind an unusual memento on the battlefield. Early in his career, before he came to Mexico, he had lost his left hand. Unwilling to give up soldiering, he had replaced it with a complicated, articulated wooden prosthesis artfully constructed to look, and function, like a hand. This he wore attached to his arm with a leather cuff. The wooden hand was found on the battlefield by a Mexican farmer and returned to the French side. Reverently carried back by the returning legionnaires, the wooden hand was given a place of honour when they were installed in their new headquarters in Sidi-bel-Abbès, and has retained, since then, the status of a holy relic.

The Second World War was an occasion for divided loyalties in the legion, but at the time of which I write, it had not yet faced its most divisive internal conflict and the bitterness of its subsequent departure from Algeria. General de Gaulle's decision to grant Algeria its independence, and consequently to withdraw France's armed forces from that country, was met with incredulous outrage. Many legionnaires joined mutinous elements in the French armed forces to oppose this move. The regular troops had their home bases in France, but North Africa was the only base the legion had and was, indeed, allowed. The legionnaires were fighting not just to maintain what they perceived as France's prestige, but to keep their home. The French left Algeria in 1962, and the legion with them. Its headquarters were established in France, in Aubagne, near Marseilles.

Reviled as much as it has been romanticised, the image of the Foreign Legion as a refuge for a rabble of miscreants and misfits still persists in some quarters. Many distinguished figures can be counted among these 'misfits' – not only brilliant soldiers but also princes and poets, writers and musicians. For its corps of officers, all of whom must be French, the legion can take its pick from the cream of the crop of graduating cadets; for aspiring legionnaires, a stringent vetting process has been in place for many decades. Legion troops receive better training; their skills and nationalities are more diverse than was the case in the first century of the legion's existence. A long-established practice of mixing companies rather than separating them by language or nationality ensures integration and prevents the formation of insular units within the legion; this has the added advantage of helping legionnaires to learn French more quickly than they might do in the isolation of a monolingual group.

A notable privilege granted to the legion is permission to deviate from the route prescribed for all other participants at the end of the Bastille Day parade on 14 July. The most colourful legion representatives at the parade are, without any doubt, the Pionniers, the sappers in their yellow leather aprons, who are the only men allowed to sport beards in an otherwise clean-shaven corps.

The Foreign Legion still serves the purpose for which it was formed – an effective and highly professional military response force that can be mobilised rapidly and can operate under any conditions – though it is now sent on peacekeeping missions rather than on missions of conquest.

In other ways, too, I imagine the modern legion is nothing like the one I knew as a young wife with Elrikh in Algeria in the '50s, and resembles even less the one in which my second husband, Aliyar, served as a very young man in North Africa in the '30s and in the Eastern Mediterranean with the Allies in the '40s. Modern transport and sophisticated equipment have changed conditions for the legionnaires, and a column of dusty men trudging along in the desert is a thing of the past.

Some things do not change, however; soldiers still sing, and an army still has to be fed. The legionnaires' favourite song is 'Le Boudin', a glorification of the hearty peasant sausage that has become the traditional meal on 30 April. On this day, legionnaires honour fallen comrades and commemorate the battle of Camerone, which first brought the Legion recognition and glory.

Chapter 6

VAL DE GRACE

Paris, 1954–1956

If my marriage had been a source of pride to my parents, my return from Algeria was something of an embarrassment to them. A daughter who had abandoned her husband, whatever the reasons, could not meet with their approval – much less one who had left him for another man. My parents quickly realised there was clearly no question of persuading me to return to Elrikh, who kept on writing enraged letters to me, and doubtless to them, vowing not to let me go.

Ali Kobakhidze, one of my oldest friends, who had been my witness and held the marriage crown above my head during the wedding ceremony, admitted to me that immediately after the wedding Papa had voiced doubts about the wisdom of marrying me off to Elrikh. Uncle Nikolai, Papa's brother and my godfather, on the other hand, had always disapproved of the match, however discreet he'd been about it, and had no doubts at all of the folly of marrying me to Elrikh. Noting my pallor during the wedding ceremony, he had taken me aside before the reception began and made me drink several glasses of champagne to put some colour, he had said, into my paper-white cheeks. The only members of my family who appeared to have had no misgivings or afterthoughts were my mother and Lia's three-year-old daughter, my niece Alexandra. She confessed many years later that, while unsupervised, she had entertained herself by emptying all the glasses that were left on the tables. She had been quite drunk, she said, by the time she was taken home.

It was quite useless to remind Papa of all this, and *Maman* was, in any case, biased in favour of Elrikh. They did not turn me away, but they did refuse to speak to me. And it was only after six months that the chilly atmosphere in the house thawed sufficiently for quasi-normal conversations to take place between us.

Their coldness felt like a slap in the face, but there was no time for brooding and self-pity. I needed to support Taïssia and myself. I had retained my figure after childbirth and had had some modest experience with modelling before I was married. This enabled me to find a job with Madeleine Colbert, who owned a small well-patronised couture house in rue Pierre 1er de Serbie, not far from the Champs-Elysées. Papa was still driving at night, which left him free for a good part of the day, and *Maman* had always worked from home, so leaving Taïssia in their care was not going to be a problem. They were more than happy to be left in charge of their granddaughter.

Lia too liked making a fuss over Taïssia. She still worked at Maison Karyinska and showed her fondness for my daughter by inviting the two of us to attend dress rehearsals whenever there was a performance she thought a child of Taïssia's age might enjoy. She had reserved a box for us once when Serge Golovine was dancing. I had known Golovine in the years before I was married. He would have been about thirty years old at this time and had been acclaimed from the time he was seventeen, so I was very flattered when he came up to the box after the rehearsal to greet me and to meet my little daughter.

There were two of us at Madame Colbert's, Denise, a brunette, and myself, fair-haired and tall. We would arrive for work at nine, and clients would generally start arriving midmorning. Depending upon the build and colouring of the client, Denise or I would model the clothes, and everybody would then take a break for lunch. Models might look languid, but it is demanding work, and between showing and fittings, we did not have any time to languish. More often than not, just as we thought we might be able to get away by closing time at six, a category of client I found particularly infuriating would arrive – ladies accompanied by husbands or lovers who, I am sure, had been badgered and bullied into accompanying them. A fresh round of showing and quick changes would begin, and on those days, I rarely got home before nine o'clock. I would be exhausted and barely able to swallow a cup of tea before throwing myself into bed.

***

My divorce proceedings dragged on. France was preparing its withdrawal from Indochina but had not yet repatriated all the regiments. André wrote to end our engagement. He had come to the realisation, he wrote, that it would be unwise for us to marry. I read between the lines and understood that it would be unwise for *him* to marry *me* – my André was an ambitious man looking for a rich wife, and I did not have the one argument that would have convinced him- I was no heiress.

I walked around in a shocked daze, saddened, even a little envious, whenever I saw a young couple, the man in uniform, his wife or girlfriend touching him constantly as if to reassure herself that he really was back – that good fortune was not to be mine. I may have been slow in finding a way of dealing with André's rejection, and lacked sufficient experience of the world to shrug it off nonchalantly, but I was determined that I would not allow the humiliation I felt to become evident to all and sundry. That was a satisfaction I would not give anybody, least of all to Elrikh, whose disdain for me had left me smarting, even though he himself was far away. Head held high but sick at heart, with my newfound self-confidence badly shaken, I concentrated on my work while considering what I should do with my life.

Renewed pressure from every side to make me withdraw my divorce petition did not affect my decision, then Elrikh wrote to my parents asking them to persuade me to join him in Algeria while he was there on leave from Indochina. The reason he gave was that he wanted to see Taïssia. No doubt existed in my mind that any meeting between the two of us could not lessen my feelings of revulsion towards him or make a difference to my decision, but I could not deny him the opportunity to spend some time with his daughter, so I went. In the light of

Ali Kobakhidze's revelation, I must admit to feeling bitter and betrayed yet again by my family.

When Elrikh and I met again, it was much as I expected it to be between us, but I was no longer the protected teenager he had married. Even if my affair with André had come to nought, I had a job and was no longer dependent upon him. This time, bullying and threats were of no avail to Elrikh. We remained equally firm in our determination not to yield ground to the other's wishes.

Whatever uncertainties the future held, they still appealed more than a life with him. I returned to Paris with Taïssia, to my job, and to the continued disapproval of my parents.

***

My colleague and co-model, Denise, and I used to patronise the Galilée, a bar-restaurant just around the corner from Mme Colbert's. It had become our regular place for lunch, and often we would look in for a drink after work as well, if we were lucky enough to get away early. As regular clients, we knew most of the staff, and I discovered I had a lot in common with the manageress, a poised woman old enough to be my mother. Her given name was Zorek, but everybody called her Zo. Her family was originally from Azerbaijan, where Russian had been widely spoken even before 1920, so it was the principal language in the household as she was growing up. She told us she had a younger brother who was with a cavalry regiment in the legion. He had been in Indochina but had been seriously wounded before the battle of Dien Bien Phu. He had been brought back to Paris and was now under treatment at Val-de-Grâce, a military hospital near Montparnasse on the Left Bank.

When Marie Seitz came back from Algeria, and rang to suggest meeting for dinner somewhere close to my work, we settled upon the Galilée as the most convenient choice. Zo came over to greet us, and after I had made the introductions, I enquired after her brother.

'He's much better now but still in Val-de-Grâce. I'm the only family he has in Paris, but I can't get away often to see him.'

Then, knowing that we were likely to react sympathetically, 'If you could find the time to visit him, it would really cheer him up.'

Visiting a wounded soldier, an elderly one at that, seemed a pretty dull prospect, and I did not have much time off, but I felt a sense of obligation to Zo, who had always been very friendly towards me. Both Marie and I also felt that, as wives of officers in the legion, we ought to make our contribution, however small. Zo gave us her brother's name and other necessary details, and Marie and I agreed to meet in front of the hospital a couple of days later, when I had a free afternoon. We were all set to spend a little while doing a good deed by cheering up a lonely, elderly man. In my own defence, I have to point out that I was just over twenty-one and Marie not much more, so anybody over thirty-five was bound to seem rather old to both of us.

Two men shared the room to which we had been directed. We explained that we were married to officers in the legion and had come to see Zo Toukaëff's brother.

'Then you're here to see me,' answered a striking-looking dark-haired man with strongly defined features.

Zo had been mischievous while describing her brother. He was indeed considerably older than we were, but there was nothing 'elderly' about him. I had just met Aliyar Bey Zulgadar, who was to become my husband. That first look was enough to make me feel as if I had been branded.

I sat next to his bed, chatting with him, my back to the door and not paying much attention to anybody else. As he gestured, I noticed that fingers were missing on one hand, and then I heard the tap-tap of crutches as a visitor entered the room. I half-turned when a man said, '*Salut Zulu,*' and then turned around completely when he continued, 'Is that how you greet an old dancing partner, Hélène?'

Surprised, I found before me a man with whom I had danced in Maskara barely a year earlier, just before he'd had to leave for Indochina. Appalled, I stared at the crutches and the pyjama bottoms that flapped emptily below both knees, and in my horror and confusion, found I could no longer remember his name (and still cannot). The rest of that visit passed between embarrassment, pity on his behalf, and a growing fascination as I watched Aliyar's effect on the entire group, sparks of the charm and energy that characterised him dancing and crackling around him like lightning. It did not turn out to be a dull afternoon after all my expectations to the contrary.

Not only was Aliyar good company, he was entirely too active for a man who had suffered extensive injuries to his chest. Restless at being confined indoors, he would sneak out. The only clothes he had apart from hospital pyjamas were his two uniforms, and he would strap up his chest and upper stomach very tightly, put on a uniform, and walk out of the hospital looking like any other officer who had been visiting an injured comrade. He was charismatic and full of life; he made me laugh, and he swept me off my feet. We met as often as we could, sometimes for a drink at the Galilée, sometimes to go to a Russian nightclub – Paris seemed to be full of them in those days – where one or other of us would invariably know the owner or manager.

***

Maman had realised that I was involved with a man, but Papa, with his odd working hours, was in complete ignorance of it until he chanced to walk into a restaurant quite late one evening. I was hungry and fancied a dish of spaghetti, so Aliyar and I had stopped in the first place we knew would still be serving food at that hour. As it happened to be Le Boudon, opposite Papa's usual stand in Place Pigalle, we should not have been surprised when he looked in for a drink.

'Don't turn around, but I think your father's just come in,' said Aliyar, as he pushed back his chair and stood up, guessing who it was as Papa spotted me and came towards us.

I was in a panic, feeling like a child caught out doing something naughty, and wanted to slide under the table as Papa approached us. Aliyar was in uniform as usual, as he possessed no other clothes. Papa was pleasant enough as I made the introductions, and Aliyar spoke to him in Russian, addressing him respectfully as Palkovnik (Colonel).

Maman told me afterwards that he woke her up when he got home and was very annoyed at having been kept in the dark.
'She's over twenty-one, Mikhail; she's a mother, a working woman, and practically divorced. You don't expect to keep her locked up at home, do you?'

What a welcome change that was from her earlier stand in favour of Elrikh. I am convinced it was she rather than Papa who had inspired their earlier coldness towards me.

***

Our affair had been going on for some months, and Aliyar and I took things day by day, when two events in quick succession forced both of us to think urgently about our future.

The first blow came when I started feeling tired and looking unwell. I underwent some medical tests. A young woman of twenty-two who feels out of sorts does not expect to be told that the state of her health is too precarious to allow her to continue working. The doctor advised me to resign immediately, maintaining that modelling was a strenuous profession. He was right; it is taxing. The tests showed that I could not afford to ignore his warning, but Taïssia and I still had to eat. The divorce had yet to go through, with Elrikh blocking it in every way he could, so there seemed to be no expectation of immediate financial relief from that quarter.

On the day of my divorce hearing, the lawyer and I were in a taxi on our way to the courthouse when he told me he'd had not had time to read the papers and prepare for the hearing. So I raced through the facts for him, talking as fast as I could before we got to the courthouse. To my immense relief, the petition was granted, and I was at long last free of Elrikh. But with regard to the future, I still felt I was back to square one.

This time I was quite devoid of ideas.

The second shock came with a further operation on Aliyar's chest, this time at the military hospital in Percy. I waited anxiously outside the operation theatre with Nasser Ali Pahlavan, the military attaché at the Iranian embassy. Paris was a desirable posting, and he was a favourite cousin of the shah.

When the attendants told us, five hours later, that the doctors were still operating, Nasser Ali burst into tears, convinced it was all over for his old friend. We hugged each other. Paradoxically, it was I, needing reassurance myself, who tried vainly to console him.

When Aliyar was wheeled out of the theatre after seven hours and we were told the results of the operation – half a lung had been removed – we knew with sinking spirits that he would not be returning to active service.

Aliyar recuperated slowly, bored and impatient to get back on his feet. He asked me to bring him canvas and coloured threads, declaring that he, like Russian generals of the past, was going to take up embroidery. I did not think he had the patience for such a sedentary activity, but to my surprise, he completed a small tapestry and asked Maman to 'finish the edges nicely' for him.

During his years in the legion, with no wife to support, Aliyar had been able to subsidise Zo, who had a chic apartment, and a large hungry dog. The butcher's bills to feed that boxer were astronomical. With little else to occupy him in Paris, he had been spending quite a bit on himself and told Zo that he could not continue helping her financially.

She was furious and, naturally enough, blamed me. She had expected her brother to amuse himself with me, not decide to marry me; I was no longer the sweet young thing Aliyar was escorting around Paris but a gold-digger who had seduced her younger brother. Anybody who knew Aliyar would have scoffed at the idea of his being seduced by a chit of a girl twenty years younger than himself, but all the same, the story did the rounds in the Russian community and came to Papa's ears. He was not best pleased, naturally.

***

I had just returned from the hospital in something of a daze after a conversation which had started with a blazing row with Aliyar. It was triggered by an incident that had taken place some days earlier. I had arrived to find a man I did not recognise, evidently a regimental comrade on leave, lounging at Aliyar's bedside.

'Meet the future Mme Zulgadar,' Aliyar said, waving a hand expansively in my direction as I walked into the room, and the rest of the introduction had passed me by in a blur. I felt humiliated, I was angry, and I had left shortly after, without having been able to talk to him in private.

When I returned a couple of days later, I told him in a fury that I found his jokes in bad taste and that I was ending our relationship.

'But, Lyenochka,[14] I was being perfectly serious. Won't you marry me?'

As a proposal of marriage, it left something to be desired. I told him that I wished he had spoken to me before announcing it so casually to anybody within earshot. I was not, of course, considering a refusal.

---

[14] Lyenochka, a diminutive of Yelyena.

I returned home to find Papa waiting for me with a grim expression, and I knew there was going to be trouble as soon as he addressed me as 'Yelyena Mikhailovna'. He only used my patronymic when he was very angry with me. He made it clear that he did not expect his daughter to get herself talked about and forbade any further association with Aliyar.

Somewhat subdued, I listened, and then explained that we had just become engaged and that Aliyar wanted to call on him. There was no telephone in the flat, so I asked for permission to go downstairs and ring Aliyar. By this time I, like Aliyar's comrades, had begun calling him Zulu. From the café opposite our building, I telephoned the hospital and told him that he had better come immediately and speak to my parents.

He arrived at the flat shortly after, having gone through the usual routine of strapping up his middle and upper body before coming out. Walking slowly up the three flights to our flat, he was received by my father, whom he addressed respectfully as *Palkovnik*. My father quite liked that reminder of what he considered his own past glories. The expected conversation took place amicably; champagne and port were brought out, and we went out to dine not far from Clichy at a favourite Russian restaurant in the 17th arrondissement. We spent a convivial evening, with Maman quite charmed when Aliyar addressed her as 'Belle-maman-belle' (beautiful mother-in-law) and Papa entirely mollified at the prospect of another military son-in-law, a much decorated and honourably wounded one at that.

As we were now officially engaged, I prepared to move out of my parents' flat to go and live with Aliyar. Zo's hostility towards me ruled out any possibility of staying with her when Aliyar was discharged from the hospital, so he rented a small flat in the 16th arrondissement. There was nothing to keep us in Paris, but we really had no idea what to do next.

Our optimism was still high, even if inspiration was more than a bit low, when Aliyar got a call from General Ali Koushishi, who had recently replaced Nasser Ali Pahlavan as Iranian military attaché. General Koushishi, also an old friend, suggested we dine with him, and a convenient date and place were fixed. There had been no hint that it would be anything more than a purely social occasion, and Aliyar was looking forward with excited anticipation to spending an evening of gossip about Iran, families he knew, and cousins and friends whom he had not seen for years.

Aliyar had always maintained such an upbeat and optimistic attitude, even when it was established that he would not be returning to the Legion, that I did not realise until much later, when I knew more about his life, to what extent he had inured himself not only to the loss in his childhood of comforts and material objects, but also to separation from cherished people and the security of familiar and beloved places. He had mentioned calling at the Hotel Plaza-Athénée to see his cousin Ninon, who was in Paris in the entourage of Queen Soraya. He had last seen the queen as a pretty unmarried girl in Iran and spoke with admiration of the poise and radiant beauty of the lovely young woman he had just met and his pleasure at her having made such a brilliant match. However, it was only after the evening with General Koushishi that I had any notion how deeply he missed his friends in Iran and the camaraderie of the legion and the army. Much later, when I myself experienced at first-hand the trauma of emotional and material loss, and the abrupt social displacement that had come with it, I could begin to imagine how profoundly he had been affected by his fragmented life.

Over dinner, General Koushishi told us that he brought an unofficial invitation from His Imperial Majesty Mohammed Reza Shah Pahlavi. The shah, aware of Aliyar's changed circumstances, suggested he might want to consider returning to Iran and to the service of the Crown. We could not, in our wildest dreams, have thought up a better solution to our dilemma.

Chapter 7

TO THE EAST

May–June 1956

Our goodbyes and extensive preparations to leave France took up so much time that I had no opportunity to ask Aliyar for reasons or further explanations for our going to Iran. I did not make an immediate connection between his visit to meet his cousin Ninon and Queen Soraya at the Hotel Plaza-Athénée and the invitation that had led to our imminent departure from France. All I knew at that stage was that Aliyar had friends at court in Tehran and that this timely invitation was the outcome of their efforts on his behalf. The how and why of it all I would learn much later. It was not a journey upon which to embark with a child, and Taïssia would remain with my parents for the time being.

We bought a Citroën, sturdy enough for the voyage and roomy enough to carry most of our luggage; the rest would follow by sea. Or so we had planned, until the arrival from Germany of Nazem Aghassipour, yet another of Aliyar's apparently infinite number of Iranian friends. He was ready to accompany us, he said, a good part of the way. He would then fly home to Tehran, while we continued in the car – with all his extra baggage.

Nazem loved gambling and had never been to the casino in Monte Carlo. It was, he pointed out, so conveniently on our way. Though Aliyar was looking forward to returning to Iran, there was no reason to deny ourselves what might be a last taste of sophisticated entertainment in a long while. Our timetable was flexible enough to allow for this short diversion, so we headed directly south. In the hills above Cannes, we found a pleasant hotel with its own car park in which we could leave our heavily laden car. It was within easy reach of the city and of the casino in Monte Carlo, and we made ourselves comfortable for what we expected would be a stay of a week at the most.

It took no more than a couple of days at the tables for Nazem to gamble away all his money; he then borrowed what we had and proceeded to lose that as well.[15] We would be obliged to spend some extra days in Cannes, waiting for fresh funds arranged by Nazem to arrive.

Aliyar, with Nazem smiling silently behind him, explained our predicament to the *patronne* of the hotel and assured her that we would shortly be in a position to settle our bill. It cannot have been the first or the last time that her guests found themselves in such a situation, as she seemed not to be too worried. She knew she could always hold on to our car, which stood in the

---

[15] Some years later, Nazem was to break the bank at the casino in Divonne.

courtyard, piled high with luggage, and I do not think she was immune to the concentrated charm of these two attractive men. Few women would have been.

We had arrived during the film festival, and Cannes was heaving with the rich, the famous, the celebrities, and the hopefuls. Nazem had been walking around with his eyes popping at the sight of so many glamorous women. He was very discreet about how he spent his time, but he was a personable man, and in spite of not speaking any French or English, he was out often and late. As he had so evidently found congenial company, we felt we could leave him to his own devices and begin to enjoy ourselves, which we managed to do quite successfully, as it turned out. Aliyar seemed to be well-known in several bars and restaurants, and their owners did not bat an eyelid when asked to grant him credit. During the Second World War, his regiment had taken part in the Allied landings on this coast, and he had spent many weeks in and around Cannes. In the course of our wanderings around the city, he pointed out a building on an extremely chic street where one of his father's divorced wives or mistresses now lived. I am not sure which it was, as in the years to come, I was to discover that the Zulgadars, father and son, shed them with the same abandon with which they acquired women.

***

We ended up spending three weeks in Cannes and set off again when the awaited funds arrived – first to Rome to drop off Nazem who would continue by air to Tehran and then on to Brindisi to catch our boat. We chose a route that took us towards

Naples in order to see Vesuvius, and I pointed excitedly as we saw plumes of vapour in the distance; Aliyar dismissed this as a complete fantasy, insisting the volcano was further south, and he would have continued without stopping if I had not shrieked and asked him crossly whether he thought all those puffs in the sky were smoke produced by a factory stack.

***

After a sea voyage, we made a stop to see friends Aliyar had made in Beirut, when he had spent part of the Second World War in that city.[16] And from there, onwards to Baghdad. I was sure something of the city's history and fabled past would remain like a lingering perfume. So much for films and fairy tales; it was thoroughly unromantic, and I could not wait to get away from its dirty brown river, its filthy streets, and its nasty smells. It had been more than ten years since Aliyar had travelled in this area, and we were advised to take the new highway through the desert. It would shorten our journey and bring us comfortably to the Iranian border.

Travelling through the desert can get quite monotonous, and the vaunted modern highway was poorly maintained. Its potholes would have slowed us down even if we had travelled by day, though we tried to travel in the cool of the night when we could. Accommodation of even the most rudimentary kind was not to be found, and by day, we would try to avoid the burning sun and would often stop to doze for a few hours in the main room of the little inns Aliyar referred to as *chai-khané*.

The Fourth Wife of Aliyar Bey

Aliyar would always go in first, and then come back for me if he felt the place was reasonably safe. It was unusual enough for a European woman to be there, let alone one in blue jeans; there were never any other women present, and among the men, we would often come across soldiers from the tented cantonments we passed.

Once, just after we had passed one of these encampments, we were flagged down by a soldier. Had we, we wondered, unwittingly broken some law, or was he about to indulge in a little banditry to supplement his income? To our relief, we had done nothing wrong, and he merely wanted to warn us of the poor condition of the road ahead. To illustrate his warning, he made generous gestures suggesting potholes the size of a fat hen.

The most memorable and beautiful sight on that journey was a desert patrol on camelback, all in dazzling white.

And through it all, like Shahryar to Aliyar's Scheherezade, I listened enthralled ...

***

It is told that two brothers lived in Baghdad in the fifteenth century; one incurred the caliph's displeasure and was condemned to death. The ladies of his household, amongst whom was a pregnant wife, were allowed to leave along with their young children and retainers. They went north into exile. The other brother, who had made his accommodation with the ruler, lost neither his life nor his goods and remained behind. The ladies stopped for a while in Turkey, and when some of them decided to continue further east towards the Caspian, others decided to remain where they were. In the first, eastbound group was the wife with her young son. Along the way, they formed alliances, made marriages, and acquired kin and the Turkish version of their name, Zulgadar.

In the Caucasus, in Azerbaijan, the family flourished; they became landowners, bred horses, grew rich, acquired property, and built a mansion in Baku. With the discovery of the oilfields there at the end of the nineteenth century, they acquired oil wells and their wealth grew. By the beginning of the twentieth century, Azerbaijan was a major producer of petrol and in the midst of an oil boom.

***

On a visit to St Petersburg, Aliyar's father, Ali Zulgadar, attended a reception at the Iranian mission where he met Mahrokh Bahador, the sister of First Secretary Assadollah Khan Assad Bahador. Ali and Mahrokh were married shortly after and had three children – Rashid; Zorek, also called Soraya; and the youngest, Aliyar (Zulu), born in Vladikavkaz in 1913. They shuttled between St Petersburg, their estates in the Caucasus, and Paris, where they maintained a house on the fashionable Avenue Henri Martin.

The Baku oilfields, Azerbaijan's greatest natural resource and the largest known deposits of petroleum at that time, proved too great a temptation for the Russians. In 1920, while still in the throes of a bloody revolution, the Bolsheviks walked into

Azerbaijan and took over the country. The bonus for them would be greater control over the Caspian and the Black Sea.

Executions followed, and thirty members of the Zulgadar family, including Aliyar's grandparents were among those summarily shot. With the help of Mahrokh's brother Assadollah Khan, at that time a highly placed official in the Ministry of Foreign Affairs, Aliyar's parents and their three children obtained Iranian passports and were able to escape on the last available ship to leave Batumi.

While her husband went to Iran to take stock of the situation and to see whether there was any hope of salvaging the family fortunes, Mahrokh and the children went to wait for him in Paris. She and Ali were divorced shortly after, but worse was to come. Mahrokh was obliged to move from the mansion in Avenue Henri Martin to a modest flat in the 15th arrondissement. She survived by cooking for those same families who had, until then, been her social peers and guests at her sumptuous receptions.

Of Mahrokh's three children, Aliyar, the youngest, was the unruliest. The high spirits of childhood and adolescence had turned to stubborn resistance when he was expected to fit into the dreary routine of his first, deskbound job. He knew he would have to find something better suited to his restless temperament and made a decision that was entirely logical – he enlisted in the Foreign Legion. It was characteristic of him not to tell his family, and like many other young men running away from home, he had lied about his age when enlisting.

Opting for the 1 Royal Etranger de Cavalerie, an élite cavalry regiment, at a time when mechanisation had not entirely done away with horses was a happy choice for somebody who missed the exhilarating freedom of those early holidays riding bareback on unbroken horses in the Caucasus. The harsh conditions in Tunisia and Morocco, where he first served, were of no consequence when balanced against the sense of having found his niche. The Foreign Legion gave him an outlet for his energy, and there was plenty of action. His individuality and wildness were assets, not the drawbacks they had been in the stifling atmosphere of an office. He had found the camaraderie that had been denied him in the uprooting and upheavals of his young life, and he got his nickname, Zulu.

Before he could complete his first five-year contract, his mother had traced him and, deeply worried for his safety, had pulled strings. Once again it was her brother, Assadollah Khan, and Prince Michel Murat, a close friend, who came to her assistance and arranged for Zulu's recall to France. Zulu was obliged to return to Paris and was not there long before he received a summons requiring him to report for national service in Iran. There was no way out of it. Furious but resigned, he left for a country he had never seen and of which he knew virtually nothing.

In spite of speaking several European languages, Zulu had not had any reason, or opportunity, to learn Farsi. As a junior officer unable to communicate with his men, he needed to be accompanied on the parade ground and in the field by an interpreter, who would shout his orders to the troops. Those few months before he had mastered enough Farsi to manage without the interpreter must have been a rare experience for all concerned.

This was in the '30s, when Reza Shah, who had been an army officer himself, was still in power. He recognised the value of having in his army an instructor with experience of modern warfare and a familiarity with modern military equipment. There was the added advantage of Zulu being an Iranian with no interest in political manoeuvring, with absolutely no reason to be sympathetic towards the Communists, and unlikely to fall prey to the seductions of any foreign power.

Disciplined enough on duty, Zulu could never resist some prank or other off duty, and if he did not always come away scot-free, neither were the repercussions too severe. This was largely because Reza Shah, who was not known for his sense of humour, was unusually indulgent of Zulu's antics. When the crown prince Mohamed Reza Shah, at that time in his teens, returned from Le Rosey, his Swiss boarding school, to attend the military academy in Tehran, Zulu was appointed to the select group of military instructors entrusted with overseeing his training.

In 1939, Europe went to war, and Zulu felt it was his duty to return to the Foreign Legion in order to fight with his old regiment; he requested leave for the duration. Assadollah Khan exercised his influence once again, this time to make sure that his nephew was denied a passport, believing, naively as it turned out, that it would suffice to prevent him from leaving. Zulu was convinced that the Foreign Legion would issue him with suitable documents, if only he could get to his old regiment. He left Iran clandestinely, persuading a boatman to row him across the Tigris into Iraq. After some misadventures, which included being locked up twice as an enemy alien, he was able to rejoin the legion in Syria in 1942.[17]

Zulu's regiment saw action in the Near and Middle East and eventually took part in the Allied landings on the Côte d'Azur. He was with the French forces when they went into Germany. He could not return to Iran, unless he was prepared to face execution as a deserter, so he remained in Germany for some years as an interpreter with various Allied forces and then did similar work for an American firm engaged in the reconstruction of the country. His older brother Rashid, for whom he did not care very much, had spent the war years in Germany, but Zulu was not very forthcoming about him.

Bored with peace and the job he was doing, he was unable to resist enlisting again when Indochina began to agitate for its independence and it became necessary for France to increase her military presence there. Happily reunited with his regiment,

The Fourth Wife of Aliyar Bey

he found himself once again in Paris, waiting to embark for the Far East. He was wounded in action and repatriated to France before the battle of Dien Bien Phu, which, politically and militarily, had been the final straw for France. The country was already preparing its withdrawal from Indochina.

If his career as a soldier in the Foreign Legion had ended painfully for him, it was not without glory. As far as he was concerned, decorations and citations for valour[18] were no substitute for the excitement of being in action or the camaraderie of the legion. Severely wounded though he had been, it was not the loss of half a lung or the two missing fingers that he regretted. However well he had concealed it, a sense of futility had overtaken him during those last months in Paris, until General Koushishi appeared like a genie out of a bottle. Zulu was being offered hope and the fulfilment of an apparently impossible wish.

On this journey, unlike during the earlier enforced departure for Iran, Zulu was eager to get there. He felt an immense gratitude towards his old pupil, now the reigning monarch, for giving him the opportunity to be active and engaged. It was a new lease on life for a man who thought his usefulness was over. He had married, and divorced, three wives in the years before we met and was now bringing home his fourth.

Chapter 8

A break from Helene's story and a discovery

Hélène's outpourings were becoming increasingly confusing. Though I had some sessions with her in the weeks that followed my work on her account so far, I found Mathilde's notes were more useful. Gaps still remained to be filled and I was feeling swamped with information I could not interpret. Also, I was confused; why was it that I could find no reference to Aliyar Zulgadar anywhere? Not in any reference books, not on the internet; I felt it was time to consult Mathilde again.

By a stroke of bad luck, Mathilde was admitted to hospital for a minor malaise, and I visited her there. She sat up in bed, looking wan and a little more dishevelled than I had ever seen her. But when I spoke of my doubts and difficulties and complained that she was taking them lightly, she smiled gaily and said, 'I think it's time for you to take a break and visit your friends in Málaga. While you're there, you could do a little research and visit Aliyar's grave in the cemetery at Benalmádena. I think that's nearby. Bring back a photograph of it, please? It would give Hélène so much pleasure. Also, there's a book that might interest you. Take a look at the pages I've tagged.'

She told me where to find the book and sent me away even more confused and mystified than I'd been when I had arrived. I located the book and packed it with my notes. Then I was off to Spain.

My ex-boss Luis was an attentive and entertaining host, and I had very little time to fulfil my commission. I did tell him about my misgivings and doubts, though.

I also read the passage that Mathilde had marked and was greatly amused by it. The memoirist's name, General Hassan Arfa, was already familiar as he figured as one of the first persons Hélène had met in Iran, an influential man, I gathered, and had given Hélène his stamp of approval, which had greatly eased her introduction to society.

Iran 1942

> Ibrahim ordered the gun to fire just beyond the crest and. calling a young cavalry captain of athletic build, introduced him to me as Captain Ali Zolqadr and ordered him to take a platoon and pursue the Kurds up to the crest of the ridge. The captain saluted and, mounting his horse, galloped off alone, forgetting in his eagerness to join the

fight to fetch his platoon. We saw him gallop past the fleeing Kurds without interfering with them or being interfered with by the panic-stricken rebels and disappear behind the crest, going directly under the shells of our guns. My brother ordered the guns to cease firing, and a platoon was sent after the captain, but before it reached the crest, we saw him through our field glasses returning with a score of armed Kurds, whom he had taken prisoner single-handed, and was driving towards the camp.

This extraordinary 'Douglas Fairbanks' of a man, of whose conquests among the European ladies of Tehran I had heard many scandalous details, was a Caucasian, the son of a millionaire horse breeder, who had emigrated during the Russian revolution to France and afterwards to Iran. He had enlisted in the French Foreign Legion and, for five years, had victimised his co-religionists in Morocco, after which he had come to Iran, where he enlisted as a specialist mechanic of armoured cars. Afterwards he was commissioned sub-lieutenant, as the Muslim immigrants from Russian Azerbaijan, which had belonged to Iran until 1828, were still considered as Iranian subjects, and had finally been promoted to captain. He had lost a front tooth in some accident, but when I suggested replacing it he confided to me that he hoped by not doing so to reduce the attentions lavished on him by the fair sex. Naturally he was a great drinker, and sometimes after emptying his glass he would chew it up and swallow it! After my brother's death he left Iran and enlisted again in the French Foreign Legion, serving in Indochina and Algeria, and after the completion of his second five-year term, married a young White-Russian émigrée and settled down in Tehran, where he is now running a restaurant and where he personally supervises the making of excellent kababs.

From *Under Five Shahs*, the memoirs of General Hassan Arfa

Of this man at least, there would be records that could be consulted; he had been influential, a soldier and a diplomat. I made a note to do that at a later date. I was somewhat encouraged by his description of Aliyar, which made me chuckle – an irresistible charmer and a man who knew his food.

Luis dropped me off at the cemetery on the day before I left, promising to be back in an hour. I had chosen red roses to put on the grave, which, together with the green foliage in which they nestled, represented the colours of the Foreign Legion. This I knew from my notes and from Hélène and Mathilde's conversations. Locating the grave became a vain search, and I sat down on a bench, puzzled and irritated. What to do now?

It had become hotter while I sat in the cemetery, and anyway, it was time for me to return to Luis. I dumped the drooping flowers in a bin on my way out. He was waiting in the car outside, air conditioning on high.

'Done your good deed for the year? Let's go and have a cool drink.'

'Oh yes, please. I couldn't find it, Luis, and there was nobody to ask. Isn't there a register somewhere to look up this sort of thing?'

My unsuccessful search had left me flustered, and I was uncomfortable in the excruciating heat.

'Do you have any other information? Oh good, a copy of the death certificate should help. Fine, I'll make a few enquiries after you've left tomorrow.'

> Some days later, I had an email that appalled me: Chère amie, the municipal office was a bit suspicious when I approached them. Who was I, and why was I making enquiries twenty years after the man's death?
>
> I assured them that I was not there to cause any trouble, but merely wanted to please an old lady by placing flowers on her late husband's grave. I said she was too old and too sick to undertake a journey, nor could she have afforded to travel here from France. I'm afraid I don't know how to put

their reply delicately. They told me that it is their policy to move the remains to a common grave after ten years, if suitable (financial?) arrangements have not been made. That is where they have put whatever was left of your legionnaire. I don't envy you having to tell those two old ladies. You told me he was in pain and died by his own hand? And now, no grave. What a sorry end!

Your old friend, Luis.

My earlier irritation and impatience dissolved, giving way to outrage and distress on behalf of a man I had never known. What a sorry end indeed.

This unfortunate piece of news and a question Mathilde had asked me – 'Wouldn't you rather read a story about a swashbuckling man than a polemic by a disgruntled politician?' – brought about a change of heart.

On reflection, she was right. I was encouraged by the thought of redressing an injustice to this unknown man in my own fashion. He may not have a grave, but I would try to give him a fitting obituary.

*****

Mathilde was sent home to La Métairie before I myself returned. I had been in such a blue funk about giving the news of the non-existence of the grave to Mathilde and Hélène that I had delayed returning directly from Málaga. I had also thought to soften the blow by presenting them with something a bit out of the ordinary when I arrived. An enlarged photograph of a substantial mansion in Baku taken at the turn of the century made an attractive cover for the folder containing my 'translation' of the first chapters. As if a pretty picture could make a difference to bad news. I had laboured over my commission though, trying to put some order into the tumble of thoughts that Hélène had spilt out, and I hoped it would garner Mathilde's approval.

***

The housekeeper took me through a spacious bedroom to a small terrace shaded by climbing roses. Mathilde sat in a wicker armchair by a table on which stood a tea tray. She looked pale in the dappled late afternoon light, and the auburn mane was not as well styled as usual. But she had dressed with care, and her eyes sparkled as she said with a chuckle, 'Chérie, how lovely to have you back!'

'You're looking well, Mathilde. I really didn't expect you to be strong enough to be sitting outdoors.'

'So show me what you have there.'

I handed over the folder and sat back. I suppose all messengers with unwelcome news feel as I did then, illogically guilty about something that is not their fault or concern and for which they certainly carry no responsibility.

Mathilde put the folder down after looking at the photograph. 'I'll look at it later. Now tell me all about what you've done. Why haven't you called at all? You're unhappy about something isn't it?'

I had long ago come to the conclusion that Mathilde's apparent frivolity was as skilfully applied as her make-up. Her mannerisms were deployed as a distraction, and the facade of a flighty fluff head concealed a keen intelligence and shrewdness; she had been, I was sure, a great asset to the late Albert in his career. At the moment, she was being more perceptive than I wanted, and I could no longer put off what I had to say.

'I couldn't find the grave,' I blurted out, going on to describe my fruitless search and Luis's discovery.

***

'Well, this is something quite out of the ordinary. How unfortunate! It certainly is an argument in favour of cremation isn't it? What a good thing Hélène's away at the moment; it'll give me some time to think about how to tell her of this.'

'Where's she gone?' I asked, feeling lighter now that I had said my piece and relieved at this unexpected reprieve, however temporary..

'She goes for an annual check-up to Robert Picqué, the military hospital in Bordeaux. They're very good about looking after their people.'

Who are?'

'The army of course. Foreign Legion and Légion d'Honneur – between them, Zulu's widow is not neglected. Now let me show you what I have for you, before we have something to eat.'

We seemed to have moved away from the subject of the grave, or rather the absence of it. I felt a surge of energy brought on by this reprieve at not having to be present when Hélène heard what I had not found and how that had come to be. Mathilde pointed to a cardboard box on a chair beside her and said, 'Open it and take a look at those. I think you'll find something more appealing than that fussy old building, whatever it is.'

I was a bit crushed at having my carefully sourced picture so airily dismissed and opened the box, which was full of photographs. Topmost was one of a couple, a young Hélène, probably in her twenties, with a much older man, strong-featured and hook-nosed. There were many more below – Hélène modelling in the '50s, which I could tell from the style of the clothes; surrounded by pigeons in Venice; squatting in front of a leopard skin; others with various people. I held up the one of the couple, eyebrows raised.

'Zulu?' I asked.

Mathilde smiled and nodded.

'And this? Looks like a dead ringer for Frank Sinatra,' holding up another that had caught my eye.

'It is the man himself, and that's Spiro Agnew next to him. They were both in Tehran when Sinatra was to sing at a charity bash organised by the Shahbanou. Hélène looks as if she's swallowed a lemon because she says Sinatra pinched her bottom just as it was taken.' She was chuckling as I held up another.

'Zulu in his Foreign Legion uniform. You know, that must have been taken when he went to the French embassy to receive the Légion d'Honneur. I've had them put on CD for you. You know the poor dear has only these left, from her parents' Paris flat. Everything else was in Tehran and went up in flames in 1979.'

And on this sobering note, we went inside.

'So my dear, are you feeling refreshed after your little holiday?' Mathilde wanted to know as we munched on tiny home-grown carrots and radishes while waiting for Hosna to bring in the rest of the meal.

'Oh yes, but I wish I had better news for both of you.'

'Let's drop the subject; it's an irreversible fact. Now tell me why you were shilly-shallying when I first brought this up. I thought you'd take it on like a shot.'

Oh dear. I did not want to insult her or Hélène by explaining those first misgivings. It was, however, an opportune moment to bring up the other reason for my initial reluctance when their project was first mooted 'Some years ago, a woman was preparing a report for my employers but had insufficient command of the language. I was delegated to help her and would go there once a week over several weeks. It was over an hour's drive each way, and I thought we could work over lunch, which I provided, but she wanted to make the meal a social occasion. She would drag it out for as long as she could. So I usually got in about an hour's real work every time I went and was so bored with her irrelevant chatter that I could barely concentrate on the important part. After we were finally done, she made a complete nuisance of herself by telephoning me at all hours to accuse me of neglecting her. Finally, I told Luis about it. He was my immediate boss then.'

'What did she really want?'

'Somebody to listen to her talk. To have mistaken professional courtesy for devoted friendship would have been easy enough for a lonely person who was no longer young and socially active. It seemed to be a harmless dependence, until the calls became drunken tirades and an intolerable nuisance. So I had to take steps to scotch them. Luis advised me to write her a firm letter. I did, and that was the end of it.'

Mathilde's expression changed as I spoke, but all she said was, 'Just shut me up if I waste your time.'

She knew I would not have dared, but we laughed nevertheless and agreed that shop talk during mealtimes was acceptable. We retired then, Mathilde to go over what I had done so far, I to listen to her recordings of conversations with Hélène and to examine the photographs.

'Why did she hate her first husband so much? She positively spits whenever she mentions him, and only slightly less when she brings up her daughter,' I wanted to know the next morning.

'She does indeed, but I don't know why. Those are private areas. Don't dwell on it; just put it down to bad chemistry. He's only a minor character.'

'And the daughter?'

'Oh, the usual, I think. Daughters with beautiful mothers often get out of hand because they believe they have something to prove. I wouldn't worry about it.'

I saw there would be no more from her on the subject, and continued, 'You've told me you liked Iran. Didn't you detect any rumblings when you lived there, some indication of deep-seated unrest?'

'Well, of course there were protests and arrests, but where in the world don't you get those? In the case of most expatriates, our experience was limited to big projects. It was easy to complain about the country without feeling any real sympathy for the people. I think as a group we saw what we wanted to see, and few had the desire or the imagination to look beyond the handsome rewards and the lavish parties.'

'Have you ever wanted to go back?'

'Not really. You know, it has become fashionable to revile the shah, but I wonder whether the people there are better off now. I realise that our occidental perspectives were quite irrelevant and most of us had neither the cultural nor the historical background to assess what we were seeing or pass judgment. What I did see was greater religious tolerance and a measure of freedom that I doubt exists today.'

'Is that why you're writing this? To set the record straight?'

'I am not qualified to analyse what happened or to write a history of the country. No, all I'm doing is telling a story. 'The writer is merely a vehicle with which to transmit information' – Zulu's friend Joseph Kessel wrote that. Think about it, Zulu's life began and ended with a revolution. The first set the course of that life. I think the second determined his last act. If it was suicide, and I believe it was, I don't see it as a defeat; I see it as wanting to have, at the end, the control that he could not exercise at the beginning and during much of his life.'

'How well did you know him?'

'A little better than purely socially, but just.'

'Handsome?'

'Depends on your definition of the word. I met better-looking men in Iran. His looks didn't matter because of his personality, and that was quite overwhelming. I'd describe Aliyar as a resourceful, charming, polished, and sophisticated man with a charismatic presence and an expansive public persona, behind which much was concealed. Deeply flawed, but how can one not be affected when one's life has been repeatedly ripped apart? I can quite see why Jeff Kessel would have wanted to write about it. Oh' seeing my confusion, 'Joseph was his given name but he was always referred to as Jeff by friends'

'Did you ever meet the Kessels?'

'No, missed them every time.'

'Flawed in what way?'

'Hmm.' She paused to gather her thoughts. 'There was the drinking, which got progressively worse; the mistresses about whom he was no longer discreet, to the point of not concealing his dalliances quite shamelessly, but one sees that kind of behaviour in varying degrees in a lot of men. He was addicted to danger, liked stirring things up, and then could not always extricate himself from the resulting damage. And he started fabulating.'

'By which you mean?'

'He would tell us an anecdote, usually autobiographical. Then, in a later version, it had snowballed into something heavily embroidered and rather more significant than the earlier version. I put it down to macho behaviour; you know how chaps can be when they're telling a story. But Hélène says that it became a serious embarrassment as the years went by. Myself, I think it was living on the edge for so long – not that it makes it any easier to live with such theatrical behaviour.'

'On the edge, how?' I was curious and wanted to get to the bottom of this.

'I think I need a little rest now. Why don't we stop for a while?'

I curbed my impatience and went for a walk around the garden while she took a short rest.

'What I'm about to tell you is pure hypothesis, conjecture based on what I observed. Hélène says that Zulu was not in uniform when he was with the army in Iran and operated out of three separate offices. And what does he do when he leaves the army? He takes up an activity that required him to travel around the country, into villages where he could make contact naturally with the people, gauge their mood. Was it a bona fide resignation? And all those restaurants, that allows for a different and equally important kind of contact. You remember the incident with the diplomat at his brother's house?'

I nodded.

'Well, that indicates pretty much what I'm suggesting. And there is, of course, his assistance to my husband and to other foreigners. I don't think it was solely goodwill that drove him. There was a reason for ensuring that those projects advanced as smoothly as possible. That took clout, and I imagine he had backing from above for what he did.'

'Given his apparent disregard for authority, how could he be suitable for the sort of thing you're talking about? I imagine you're suggesting he was connected with an arm of national security or intelligence in some way?'

'Consider this: In Iran, the Communist movement was the one most feared by the Crown. Zulu had every reason to be loyal to a man who had given him a pardon and made him feel he was doing useful work. He and Hélène's families had lost everything to the Communists and had no love for them, be they Iranian or Russian. So His Majesty had every reason to trust both husband and wife and to be certain that they would have nothing to do with any group that aimed to destabilise the regime. Not that I think she was directly involved in any way, but she must certainly have suspected what he was doing. And then there is the matter of his last years. There is no logic in his going to Spain when he could very easily have remained in France, where he had friends and a network through the Foreign Legion. But there was, and still is, a large community of exiled Iranians where he settled. Some of them were influential figures in Iran and consequently were, maybe still are, close to what's left of the royal family. I think that may have been a decisive factor in his going there. In the feudal sense, and Iran was still very feudal then, I think he never left His Majesty's service at all.'

This was quite a lot of information to take in over a day, and I had no way of knowing whether Mathilde's assertions were correct. At any rate it was not for me to corroborate them. I decided to satisfy my curiosity about something else that nagged at the back of my mind, and asked 'What about Dick Duparc and his wife? Why does she call them fair-weather friends?'

'When she returned to France, she was desperately in need of money and a job. A large industrial company like the one Dick worked for always has openings, and he was in a position to have found her something. Just to survive, you understand, nobody's talking of a high-profile position with a fat salary. Well, he didn't do a thing for her or for Zulu later. They'd served their purpose and had become expendable, no longer placed to further the husband's professional ambitions or the wife's social aspirations.'

With this scathing observation of the Duparcs, she brought our conversation to a close for that day.

Chapter 9

PERSIA BECOMES IRAN

As the seven-year-old Aliyar fled Azerbaijan with his parents and siblings, an upheaval which would topple the reigning Qajar dynasty was under way in neighbouring Persia.

When Persia entered the twentieth century, it was a country in need of modernisation, with medieval institutions and virtually no infrastructure. Of its three imperial neighbours – the Ottomans to the West, the Russians to the north, and the British controlling the Indian subcontinent along the southern half of Persia's eastern frontier – it was these last two whose growing influence during the second half of the nineteenth century was watched by Tehran with mounting concern. After the mutiny of the Indian troops, Britain's contemptuous treatment of the Indian ruler Bahadur Shah Zafar was not reassuring, and neither was Russia's treatment of her tsar. Moreover, ever greedy to expand, Russia was looking to acquire warm-water ports on the Indian Ocean, and Britain was determined to thwart such ambitions by any means. With both powers intent upon pursuing their 'Great Game' on its territory, Persia had to depend upon diplomacy and played off one against the other in order to escape being annexed or colonised by either. It was too weak, however, to prevent their interference in its internal affairs. Tribal divisions and rivalries could be, and had been, exploited by both parties to this end; by the beginning of the twentieth century, vast areas of the country were only nominally ruled from Tehran.

By 1909, successive shahs had obtained loans for their personal use from both the Russians and the British, granting in exchange fishing rights, trading concessions, and future revenues. They had ratified a constitution and then tried to re-establish the earlier absolute power of the monarchy by terrorising the newly formed *majles* (parliament). Civil unrest and popular demand for political reform had been answered with such savage repression by the ruling monarch, Mohammad Ali Shah Qajar, that they led to uprisings and revolts bloody and violent enough to force him to abdicate in favour of his minor son, Ahmad Shah. Persia had a child on the throne, an ailing regent, a fledgling parliament, and a growing foreign debt.

All this might have been of no more than passing interest to the world at large if oil had not been struck in 1908. The stakes had been raised, and it was no longer a question of who collected revenues from caviar or tobacco but of a precious resource for which nations went to war. For Russia, it was galling that the concession for the exploration and production of petroleum had already been granted in 1901 to William Knox d'Arcy, a British subject, well before the actual discovery had been made by his team of French prospectors. For Persia, the discovery brought the hope of sufficient wealth to modernise the country, to develop its industries, and to strengthen it against external interference. The government turned to the United States for assistance in reorganising its finances, believing that only a strong international power could provide a counterbalance to the Anglo-Russian stranglehold upon the country. Morgan Shuster from the United States was appointed to reorganise the government's finances.

Russia was perceived as the greater threat, and there was, consequently, a pro-British bias. This changed just after the First World War, when a secret agreement carving up the country between Russia and Britain came to light. Britain had, moreover, succeeded in making sure that a Persian delegation to the Paris Peace Conference of 1919 be denied a hearing. The general humiliation and sense of outrage that were felt in the country had bred open hostility towards Russia and Britain and brought both powers to the realisation that they would have to tailor their strategies to the new political mood in Persia. Discretion was called for. The First World War and the 1917 revolution had greatly weakened Russia. Taken up with its internal problems and continuing power struggles, it could not afford to concentrate the same attention or divert the same resources as it had earlier done to maintain its powerful presence in Persia. The way lay open for Britain, but greater circumspection and different tactics would be required if it was to retain its influence in the region.

The Qajar dynasty had been on the throne of Persia since 1794, when its founder, Agha Mohamed Khan, triumphed over his rival chieftains after a long period of bloody intertribal struggles. Ahmad Shah, the seventh Qajar ruler, was twelve years old when he came to the throne after his father's abdication in 1909; in 1920, he was still young, inexperienced, and somewhat frivolous. Corruption was rife, ministers came and went, power shifted between constitutionalists in favour of a parliamentary model of government, and conservatives in favour of the status quo. Perhaps it was time to make a clean sweep of it and for that, new blood was needed – somebody with no ties to the moribund old regime and no vested interest in upholding it.

Reza Khan, a senior officer in the Persian Cossack Brigade[19], had risen from the ranks, was well-regarded by his superiors, and had displayed courage and the qualities of leadership; he was, in short, a suitable choice to lead a coup. It is widely believed that what followed was brought about with the connivance of Britain – could not, in fact, have been successful without it.

Reza Khan acted decisively and rose swiftly to power. By 1921, he was commander-in-chief, a post he combined with that of minister of war. By 1923, he was prime minister, and by 1925, he had engineered a coup while the shah was away

---

[19] In 1878, Nasser al Din Shah Qajar had been greatly impressed by Tsar Alexander III's Cossacks, and a Persian Cossack Brigade was established under a forty-year agreement with Russia. Its senior officers were Russian, and Persia provided the manpower. It functioned mainly as a royal bodyguard, until the First World War, when it was enlarged and Persian officers were promoted for the first time to senior positions, though still under a Russian commanding officer. The brigade played a decisive role in the coup that brought Reza Khan to power and was later absorbed into the national army.

on a European jaunt. In 1926, Reza Khan was crowned Reza Shah and adopted the surname name Pahlavi. It was not until 1935, however, that he decreed that Persia would henceforth be known as Iran, a name that resonated with the glories of an ancient empire.

Ahmad Shah never returned to the country of his birth, and is buried just outside Paris. The rule of the Qajar kings had come to an end after a hundred and thirty years on the throne of Persia. This time, it was incompetence and a weak, corrupt government, rather than the intertribal rivalry of earlier times, which had paved the way for a change of government and a new ruler. A large segment of the population supported Reza Shah's accession to power. This included some of the clergy, who were alarmed by Communist-inspired secessionist movements in the northern parts of the country, and the *bazaris* or tradesmen and merchants, weary of the rioting and unrest, which was bad for business. Even within the ruling class, among those who had every reason to expect an abrogation of their privileges, there were progressives who saw the need for a leader capable of establishing a strong central government able to implement policies that would bring the political and economic stability required to keep the country free of external influence and take it forward. The tribal khans would be among those most affected by his vision for the country, which would inevitably result in a limitation of their autonomy. Bringing these formerly autonomous leaders under the control of the centre was Reza Shah's first task.

The government then undertook a sweeping programme to modernise the country. From extending the limited network of railroads to developing the mining industry and from establishing universities to installing telecommunications, a variety of projects were initiated. Public health and education were given the highest priority; hospitals were built. And until such time as academic institutions with a sufficiently high standard of instruction could be established, scholarships were made available for young Iranians to be trained abroad in every discipline. Though the royal family were known to be devout Muslims, when Reza Shah passed a law obliging women to discard the veil, the royal ladies appeared in public in Western dress and without a veil, with the intention of setting an example that would serve to demonstrate that religion and progress were not mutually exclusive. Persuading traditionalists to follow this last directive proved particularly difficult, and the army had to be called out[20] to ensure that it was enforced. Many of these initiatives met with resistance, if not active hostility, from the clergy who had earlier supported him and now foresaw in them the diminishing of their own power.

There were others who, while agreeing with the need for change, felt that the pace could not be forced and were eliminated for being outspoken on the subject. Yet others were eliminated because they were perceived by Reza Shah as a threat to his newly founded dynasty. 'To drink the shah's coffee' became the common euphemism for those who, having fallen out of favour, had been eliminated without recourse to bloodshed.[21]

It was, eventually, not the clergy but the Allies who forced Reza Shah's abdication in 1941 and placed his eldest son, Crown Prince Mohammed Reza, on the throne. The Allies proposed using Iran's Indian Ocean ports to supply Russia with urgently needed war materiel, which would be transported overland on the newly completed Trans-Iranian Railway to the Caspian ports and the Russo-Iranian border. In order to guarantee the safe passage of these supplies, they also proposed taking over control of Iran's armed forces for the duration of the war.

Reza Shah had retained a deep-rooted suspicion of the British and the Russians and their motives with regard to his country. He acknowledged the need to cooperate with the Allies, but not to the extent of handing over command of his armies to them. He had no intention of becoming anybody's puppet and remained firm in his determination to maintain Iran's neutrality and its sovereignty. Any other course of action would negate the reasons for removing the Qajar kings and taking power for himself.

The Allies suspected senior officers in the Iranian army of pro-German leanings, and Reza Shah himself was thought to be like-minded. It should be noted that though this was more

---

[21] Coffee is served to indicate that a conversation or a meeting is over. Here, it indicated the end of the man's life, usually by forcing the man to drink a fatally drugged coffee.

often than not an expression of anti-British or anti-Russian sentiment rather than of any actual support for Germany, it was enough to provide convenient grist to the mill of the Allied propaganda machine. If there was any danger of Iran, with its gigantic oil reserves and strategic position in the Gulf and Indian Ocean, falling within Germany's sphere of influence, the Allies would prevent it by any means they could. It was Reza Shah's turn to go.

Reza Shah went into exile after the Allies bombarded the ports of Khorramshahr on the Indian Ocean and Bandar Pahlavi on the Caspian, completely destroying the Iranian navy. The demoralised army put up a feeble token resistance[22] to a clearly superior foe, and the way was open for the Allied occupation of Iran. It lasted from 1941 until 1945.

Reza Shah died in Johannesburg in 1944. His remains were eventually brought back to Iran in 1950 and transported in state to be interred near a holy shrine at Rei, a small town not far from Tehran. Autocratic and unyielding, Reza Shah had given Iran the sense of direction and the impetus that had been lacking when he came to power. He was a man in a hurry to bring Iran into the twentieth century and would brook no disagreement as to timing and method in his efforts to achieve that end.

---

[22] According to General Arfa in *Under Five Shahs*, this was a political decision designed to appease the Germans, in the event of their being victorious.

It had been thirty years since he had set Iran on its new path; Hélène and Zulu had almost reached Iran and were about to see how successfully his successor had achieved the goals Reza Shah had set and what fruit his legacy was bearing.

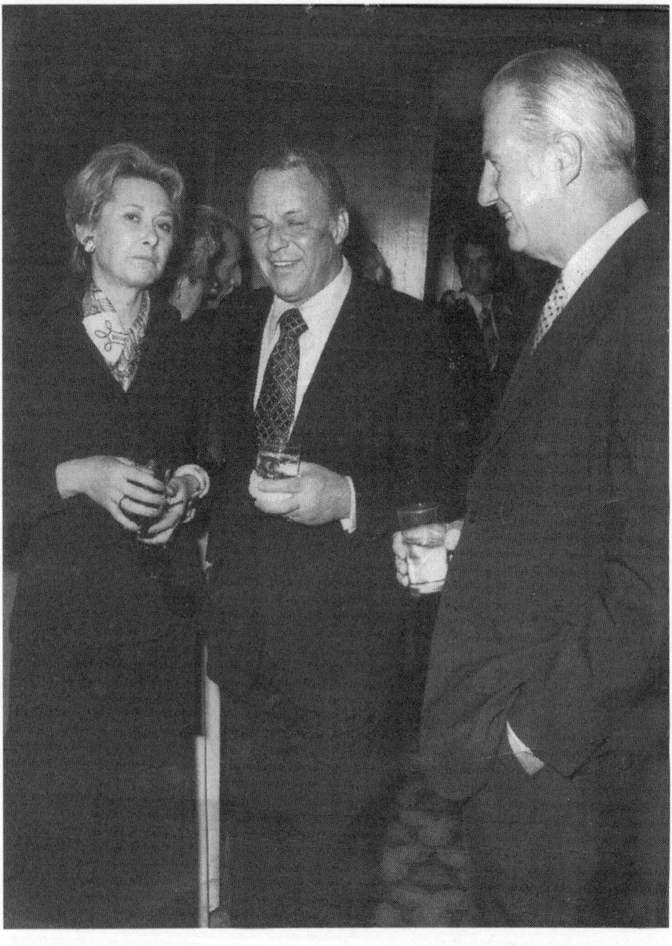

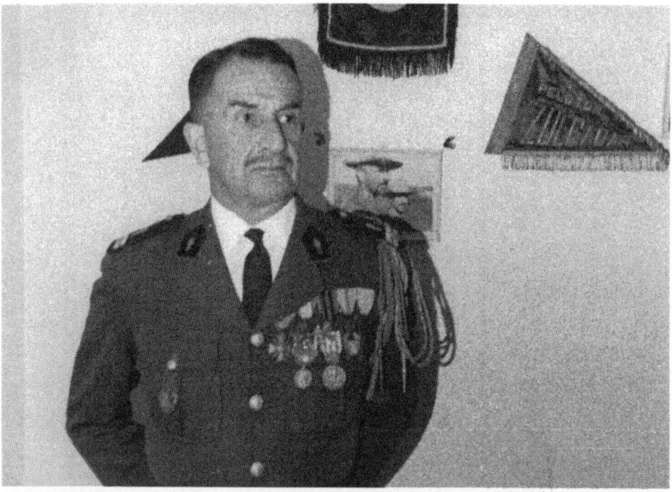

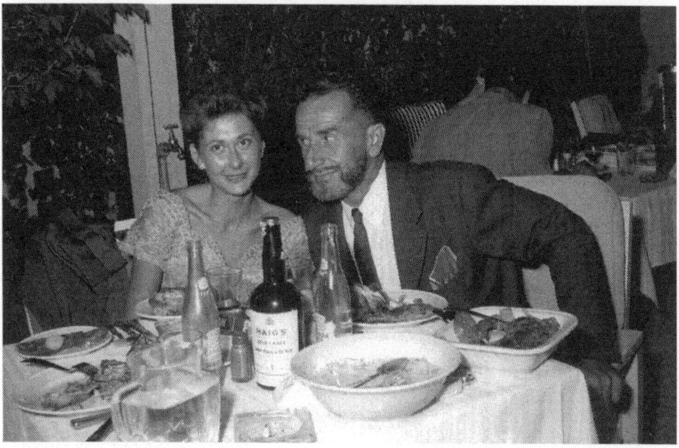

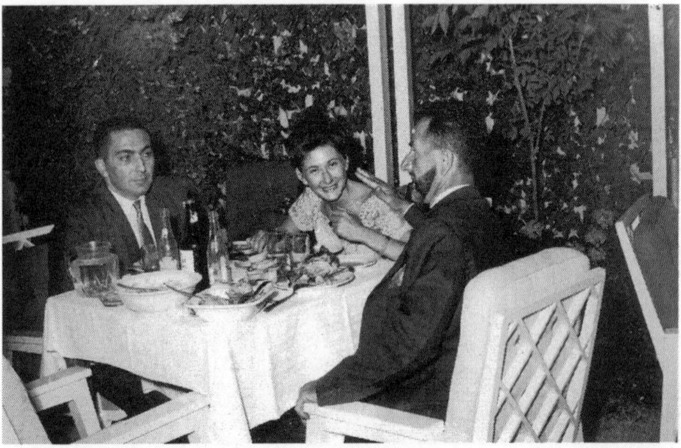

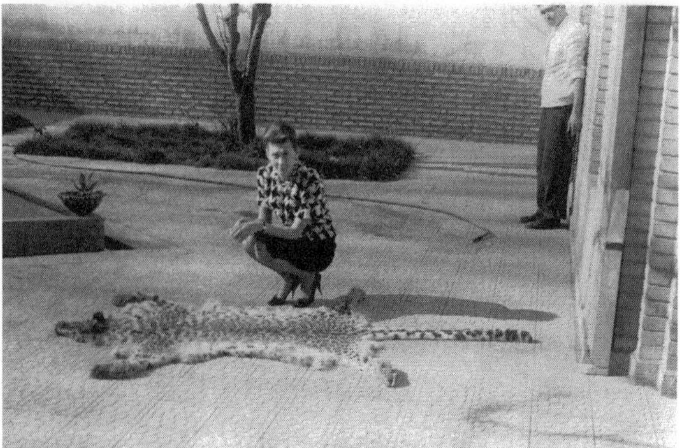

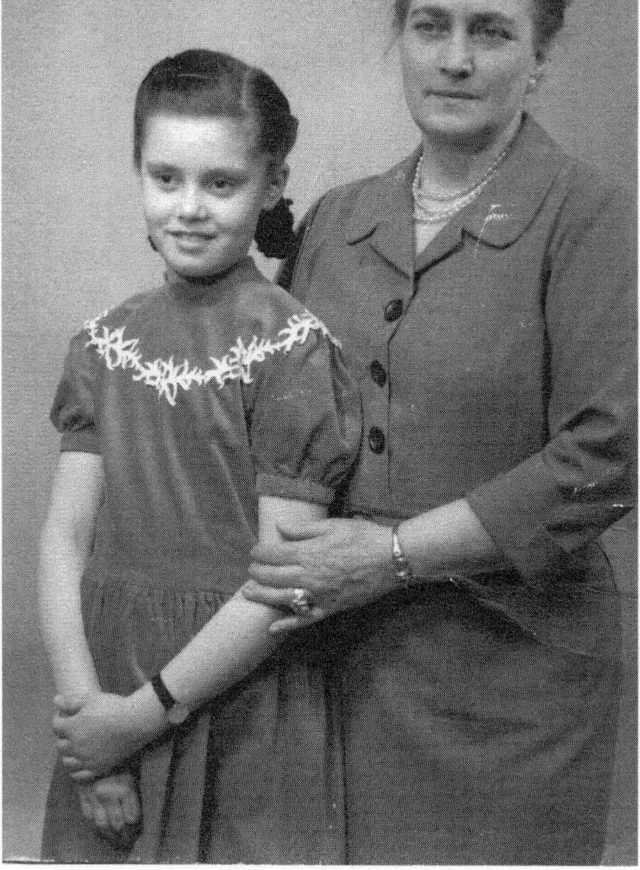

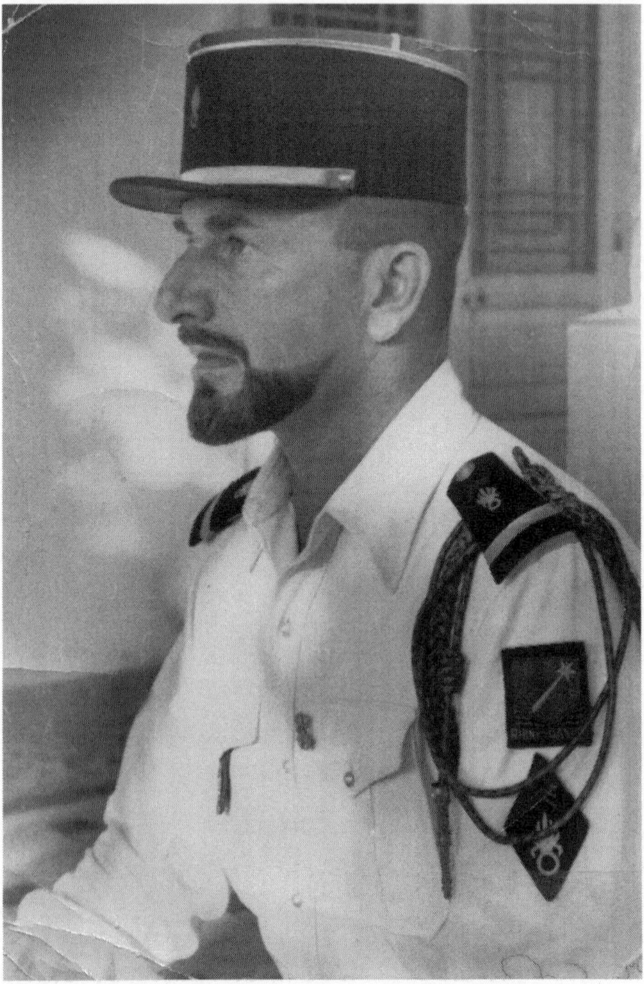

Chapter 10

HELENE CONTINUES HER ACCOUNT

Arrival in Iran
May 1956

Technically Zulu was still a deserter from the Iranian army. His reasons for leaving the country in 1943 had been honourable enough; he'd wanted to stand and fight with his first and earliest comrades. He also believed that, by rejoining the legion, his abilities were of greater use to both the Allies and to Iran. Perhaps he'd hoped his actions would be seen in a benign light and that all would be forgiven after the war was over. But he had, whatever the outcome, been prepared to suffer the consequences of leaving the country and the Iranian army without permission to do so. We were not sure who was privy to the unofficial 'invitation', and if instructions to the contrary had not been issued, there was a strong likelihood of his being imprisoned as we entered the country. So we were rather nervous as we approached the frontier post and joined the long line of vehicles waiting to cross over from Iraq to Kermanshah on the Iranian side.

Zulu handed over our papers and was asked by the frontier guard to come into the customs building.

'Don't leave the car; don't open your mouth,' he said as he got out to follow the man – quite unnecessary, as I had no command of Farsi, other than the few polite phrases he had taught me. The unfamiliarity of everything was overwhelming. Ancient overloaded ramshackle lorries carried cartons of sophisticated modern consumer goods. Buses overflowed with bundles, unruly children, and men and women in shalwar kameez; very few women covered their faces or wore chadors. Everywhere I looked was a bustle and a noise.

I waited fearfully in the car for close to an hour until the guard came out of the building and indicated politely that I should follow him. I did not have any choice, so I did as I'd been bid. We entered a large hall where people were opening up suitcases and bundles for the customs inspectors. My heart sank as I thought of the number of suitcases, ours and Nazem's, that would have to be unloaded, opened, checked, and reloaded. Still no sign of Zulu and the guard continued towards the rear of the building where he came to a stop before an office. Zulu sat there surrounded by half a dozen men, army and customs officials judging by their uniforms, all holding glasses of tea or soft drinks and looking quite jolly. It did not look to me as if this was the prelude to an arrest, but I had no way of knowing that with any certainty when I joined them.

The men greeted me as Khanum-e-Zolqadr, and though I did not understand Farsi, I knew this was the appropriate form when addressing a married woman. After I had brought out my few Farsi courtesies, Zulu and I did not have to wait long before we were on our way, waved through with broad smiles and without any inspection of our luggage. Far from wanting to arrest him, they were thrilled to see 'Ali Zolqadr', as he was known to them, and had kept him back wanting to hear about his escapes and escapades, the war and the Legion, Indochina, and his wounds. After we had left them, Zulu explained to me that 'Zolqadr' was the Iranian version of the family's Turkish name 'Zulgadar'. He also explained that, if everybody thought we were already married, there would be no need to duck awkward questions or give lengthy explanations.

We were quite chuffed; we had come through the desert without mishap and had been welcomed into Iran. The most difficult part of the journey, we believed, was over; when the Citroën's brakes failed while negotiating a series of hairpin bends down from the mountains, we found it hilarious, if somewhat inconvenient. I would get out of the car and skip down to meet it at the next bend. A couple of days later, we were close enough to Tehran to want to press on without stopping for the night.

Night-time, and changes to the city over more than a decade made everything unrecognisable. After driving around in circles for over an hour, Zulu finally admitted he could no longer find his way home and hailed a taxi to lead the way. In the early hours of the morning, we drove into the courtyard of the house and woke up everybody. It mattered little that the hour was unsociable; the son of the house was home.

My future father-in-law, Ali, shared the house with his two widowed sisters and a nephew. Zulu's aunts spoke Farsi, Turkish, and Russian but no French. His cousin Ilkhan Zelli was an engineer, and it was Ilkhan's job with a foreign company that kept the household afloat. Ilkhan's younger sister, Malek, was studying abroad.

Unable to communicate in French, our common language was Russian. No language was needed, however, for me to recognise the instant and intense dislike they did not bother to hide. Their principal objection appeared to be based on my being an Orthodox Christian. Religious differences had been no bar to frequent intermarriage between Iranians and Russians, so it was hard to understand why they reacted in this way. Perhaps Zo's letters had influenced them, or perhaps they had envisaged an entirely different sort of wife for Zulu; an alliance with a well-connected and influential family might have met with their approval.

Whatever the reasons for their hostility towards me, they managed to make those first months in the Zulgadar mansion quite uncomfortable – unpleasant enough, in fact, for me to want to block out as much as possible of that time. Ilkhan's mother was Aunt Shouket, but I have now forgotten what the other aunt was called. They were aided and abetted by Zeenat, the fat and slovenly cook.

An early incident that remains in my memory is my alarm at the disappearance of my newly issued identity card. Even though I was under Zulu's protection, Iran was not a country in which to be found without the right papers. In growing panic, I looked everywhere, even in the dustbin. There lay the card, with thick black strokes inked all across my photograph – I was wearing a small cross on a chain around my neck when it was taken. Impossible to know who was responsible for this act of destruction, but that I was not welcome in the household was clear.

Zulgadar père was still a fine figure of a man in his early seventies, and I saw a marked resemblance between father and son. He had studied law, but what he did after he lost his lands and most of his wealth and how he had spent the years before we arrived are a mystery to me. From what I could see, he led a life of complete indolence. Though he had not had a wife for some years, I do not think he ever lacked for the company of women. As he, together with the rest of the household, thought I was already married to his son, I was viewed as a daughter-in-law and relegated to the background, so I was not required to have much to do with him, which suited me very well, as I had not taken to him.

The house was in an old quarter of Tehran, down one of the narrow streets known as *koucheh*. Hidden behind a high wall, it was built in the traditional style, with a courtyard in front and a garden at the back. Though my memories of it are not very happy, in the months following our arrival, Zulu introduced me to a circle of friends and extended family whose welcome more than compensated for the lack of warmth towards me in that house.

Fathollah Amir Alahi and Zulu had known one another from the time Fathollah had been sent to study in Paris by his father, an admiral in what was still the Persian navy. He had been treated as a member of the family by the Zulgadars and had spent all his free time with them at Avenue Henri Martin. The two boys had become, and still remained, fast friends. Fathi, as everybody called him, was trusted by the shah, had become administrator of the royal properties, and wielded considerable influence. He was also a good-looking man and one of the most sought-after escorts in Tehran. He would invite me to accompany him when he went on an inspection in or around Tehran, and I came to know the city and its surrounding areas quite well. He was as aware of the unconcealed hostility of my in-laws towards me and of the discomfort I felt in that household, as he was of our strained financial situation. He would manufacture opportunities for us to be out of the house and ring us with an impromptu invitation to see a film or try out a new bar or café or to accompany him to a popular restaurant in the bazaar, reputed for its kebabs. We were both to turn to him in times of need, and his staunch support and concern for our well-being never

The Fourth Wife of Aliyar Bey

wavered throughout my years in Iran. He also introduced me to an Iranian custom that I found comforting. I suffered from migraines, and when I wanted to take to my bed one day, he recommended an indigenous remedy and handed me a small, slightly sticky golden ball, which I was supposed to swallow. It worked its magic on me and he told me afterwards that it was opium, 'the best quality, my dear, which you'll recognise by its colour; don't ever accept anything inferior.'

I learnt that it was the custom in Iran to consume it in modest quantities. In the evenings, when the men gathered for a discussion and a chat, usually at somebody's house, they would be seated on carpets in two rows on either side of the host; as the evening advanced, a servant would bring in a covered tray on which these golden balls were set out. The host would take one, after which the servant would go around offering the tray to every man present.

Fathi did not look at all dozy after consuming his share that first time, so I concluded it was quite safe. I was also delighted to have found a natural and easily accessible remedy for the headaches, which had been plaguing me for years and often laid me low.

***

Shortly after Zulu had been informed that he would be rejoining the army with the rank of brigadier general, we were invited to a lunch party given by General Hassan Arfa at his estate in Niyavaran just outside Tehran. Zulu had first met the general in the 1940s, while serving under his brother Ibrahim.[23] Though the general had retired from the army, I understood that this occasion would be more than a mere courtesy call by a junior officer. Held in great respect by all, the general was a widely travelled man who had been trained as a cavalry officer; had been responsible for the reorganisation of the Iranian cavalry; and had also been, among other things, chief of staff during the course of his long army career before he became a diplomat. He had often represented Iran at international conferences and was later sent as ambassador to Turkey, and then to Pakistan.

We had been instructed to arrive early so that I could be 'properly' introduced. The general's house seemed to me very old, and the grounds must have been extensive, or so I imagine, because after the introductions and greetings warm enough for me see both men were genuinely pleased to be meeting again, the general sent Zulu for a ride around the estate, saying he wanted to talk to me. After the operation on his lung, Zulu had been advised not to ride again, but this was in the nature of an order, and an opportunity he could not resist.

General Arfa then took me for a stroll in the garden before the other guests arrived, my arm tucked under his, within view of the house but out of earshot.

---

[23] Brigadier General Ibrahim Arfa, General Hassan Arfa's brother and Zulu's commanding officer, died in a plane crash in 1943, and Zulu 'deserted' shortly after that.

The general was a slender man and had kept the fit and well-tanned look of a man who has spent the major part of his life outdoors and on horseback. He spoke fluent French, and through his mother and maternal grandmother, both of them Anglo-Russian, fluent English and Russian as well. Mrs Arfa, who was English, had been a member of Serge Diaghilev's Ballets Russes when she and the general met in Monte Carlo in the 1920s.

I knew that this was a vetting, but his avuncular manner immediately put me at my ease. He asked about my family, Elrikh, Algeria, and our recent journey. He then started talking about the Cossacks, about the Côte d'Azur as he remembered it, and what to expect from life in Tehran. I can still hear him saying, 'From the twenty-first of September, the temperature drops by a degree every day, and you'll see snow for Christmas.' It turned out just as he had predicted.

I was enjoying our chat but did not want it thought that I was monopolising the host. When I mentioned that I could see his other guests arriving, he simply patted my hand and continued walking, pointing out this flower or that tree. Our stroll lasted almost an hour, after which we returned to the house to join the others, who were being entertained by Mrs Arfa. Over lunch, which was an alfresco buffet laid out in the shade of a spreading tree, I was intrigued to observe that, far from playing the grand lady, she was rather self-effacing and looking constantly towards her charismatic, lynx-eyed husband for approbation.

I understood that the purpose of the walk had been to provide a very public demonstration of the general's approval of Zulu's wife, and I was grateful to him for it. Some curious and not entirely friendly looks were cast my way throughout the afternoon, but the general had set the tone for the people who were there. I was more readily accepted after that occasion.

We did not see much of him after that, as he left shortly after to take up a diplomatic posting. Years after that lunch, I was interested to read his short and accurate observations about Zulu in his memoirs; in an anecdote, he describes Zulu's impetuosity as a young officer serving under his brother Ibrahim. That characteristic had not been greatly tempered by the years, and neither, I would discover as time passed, had many other traits.[24]

***

Zulu's cousin Ilkhan had been the only one in the family to show any warmth towards me, and both of us wanted him to be present at our wedding. After we had completed the necessary formalities and fixed a date, we asked him in confidence to take the day off work without telling him why. The three of us slipped away without a word to anybody in the household, and, accompanied by Nasser Ali Pahlavan, who was now back in Tehran, and General Ali Khazayi, all five of us presented ourselves at the office of the mullah, who, among other things, functions as a religious notary, solemnising and registering marriages.

---

[24] General Hassan Arfa, *Under Five Shahs*, (New York City: William Morrow & Company, 1965), 311–312.

Zulu, Ilkhan, and General Khazayi were called in first and held a discussion with the mullah, while Nasser Ali and I waited in another room. When we were called in, I found it rather strange that my husband-to-be would not be present at the marriage ceremony and that, in the absence of any male member of my family, Nasser Ali was to give me away. It was quite odd to hear Zulu and the other two laughing in the next room, but, giving a mental shrug, I followed Nasser Ali's instructions, which were to say *balé* (yes) whenever he told me to. I tried to look suitably demure and keep a straight face as, in a barely audible voice, he translated the ceremony for me into choice Parisian argot.

I was first declared a Muslim and given the name Elahé, which we had chosen for its resemblance to Hélène. Then, after having said yes in Farsi a few more times, whenever I was prompted to do so, I was told that I was now married. Zulu and the other two had been playing cards to pass the time, and when they joined us, the five of us drove away in a state of high hilarity. I found the proceedings refreshingly uncomplicated in a country bound by tradition and bureaucracy – Hélène Ponomareff had been renamed Elahé and become the fourth wife of Aliyar Bey, entitled to call herself Beghum Zulgadar, all in the short space of an hour.

This signing of a contract in a starkly furnished office may sound a little flat. There were none of the trappings that demonstrate to the world the joyous nature of such an event – no fine wedding dress, no flowers, no ornately decorated church, no reception, no popping of champagne corks. There had been an abundance of these when I married Elrikh, and everybody else present on that day had, it seemed, something to celebrate. Even Lia's three-year-old daughter, my niece Alexandra, had enjoyed the occasion. I was, it seemed, the only one who had felt like a garlanded sacrificial goat; this second time, dressed in a simple blue cotton dress against the summer heat, far from anyone or anything familiar, with no pomp whatsoever, I was married to a man I loved and was elated by the knowledge.

That evening we marked the occasion by going out for an intimate dinner à deux. Naturally, we had to conceal the reason for our celebration from the rest of the household, but there was no reason to hide the happiness we both experienced.

After that, I was ready to be introduced officially to a more exalted stratum of society. Zulu was fonder of his cousin Ninon, the daughter of his maternal uncle Assadullah Khan Assad Bahador than he was of his siblings; Ninon looked up to him as the older brother she wished she could have. It was, therefore, natural that he turned to her for help. She was to present me to the 'inner circle' – the ladies of the royal family and the favoured companions who made up their entourage.

Chapter 11

NINON

The early 1900s and later

As a young diplomat, Ninon's father, Assadullah Khan Assad Bahador, had spent twenty years in Russia. At that time, Russia still boasted a glittering imperial court and St Petersburg was a desirable posting. The blood-soaked years between 1917 and 1920, the murder of Tsar Nicholas and his family, the unconcealed political ambitions of the Bolsheviks, and their summary disregard for Azerbaijan's sovereignty made Persia, already wary of its powerful neighbour, alert to the need for stronger diplomatic ties with the nations of Europe.

After the First World War, Assadullah Khan was appointed ambassador to France, and he and his aristocratic Polish wife, Lili, were in Paris when their daughter Ninon was born. The family was installed at the Claridge Hotel while waiting for the official ambassadorial residence to be made ready; Ninon was born there. It was an unusually swanky address, I thought, to have on a birth certificate. When Assad Bahador returned to Tehran at the end of that posting, he was appointed court minister. While still in Paris, the story went, Uncle Assad had a specially installed telephone line in his toilet, in order to have chats with his mistress.

When the family was back in Tehran, Ninon and the young crown prince, both in their teens, developed an adolescent attachment for one another; he let it be known that he wanted to marry her. Her background and lineage were no bar to what would have been a brilliant match, but her father is reported to have disapproved on the grounds that he would not allow his daughter to marry one whom he called a usurper's son. To have said this loudly or publicly would have brought grave repercussions upon the whole family, so doubtless some suitable reason was proffered for his refusal to entertain the Crown Prince's proposal.

Prince Mohamed Reza married Princess Fawzia of Egypt but remained on good terms with Ninon. She was one of the few companions of his youth whose company he called upon regularly when they were both adults. He liked to spend a sociable evening or relax over a few rubbers of bridge with her.

Ninon eventually married Felix Aghayan, who came from a well-established family of Armenian origin. Felix's father, Alexander, had been an international lawyer, but he himself was a successful businessman and later a senator, leaving his brother, Shahine, to follow in their father's footsteps and take over his legal practice.

In the post-war years, the shah launched an initiative to transform Tehran into a city to match, if not rival, European capitals. Oil money was everywhere in evidence, and shops carrying luxury goods of every imaginable variety were opened. Those who could afford it – and many could – flew to Europe to shop, more often than not to Paris. Others thought nothing of having a meal flown out from Maxim's in Paris. Not only for its cuisine but for everything else too, Paris was the source of all that was desirable. The city was considered the Mecca of high fashion, with Christian Dior as its high priest. Ninon, no stranger herself to the haute couture salons of Paris, approached Mr Dior with a proposal to bring his creations to Tehran's upper crust on a very exclusive basis.

That Ninon was well-placed to make a success of such a venture was in no doubt, and she was able to return to Tehran with two senior cutters from the house of Dior in tow. Always addressed as Monsieur Pierre and Mademoiselle Laguy, they supervised a team of seamstresses and embroidery women who were hired locally and installed in workshops set up in an elegantly appointed house on Pahlavi Avenue. Monsieur Pierre was in charge of what were called structured clothes, suits, and the like, whereas mademoiselle's domain was the fluttery and supple.

Pahlavi Avenue was a broad tree-lined street that runs from the centre of the city all the way to the cooler heights of Shemiran. A chauffeur-driven car had been sent to bring me there. We stopped outside a substantial house, which gave directly onto the street with a small brass plaque set into the wall next to the door; it read quite simply *Ninon*, with no further indication of what lay beyond it.

A visitor would be received in the spacious foyer and taken to one of the reception rooms on either side. These three rooms were decorated in the signature colours of the house of Dior, pale grey with white and gold trim. The atmosphere was one of velvety luxury, designed to pamper and persuade, to affirm to the privileged and the rich just how privileged and rich they were. This was where the fashionable ladies of Tehran came when they wanted a chic outfit, a beautiful dress, or simply to be cosseted and tempted. Sometimes they would come to find out what was being worn in Paris, sometimes in the hope of finding out what other women in their circle would be wearing. They would sit over tiny cups of coffee while looking at the swatches of fabrics accompanying drawings of the latest models, admiring one or dismissing another, exchanging the latest gossip all the while.

It had been just over twenty years since Reza Shah had decreed that women were to give up the veil and could move about freely, and though these modern ladies would have been outraged at the removal of these liberties, the habits of an old and established culture are not easily put by. The atmosphere here resembled one in which the ladies were still most comfortable, that of the *anderoon*[25] of a wealthy household.

---

[25] Women's quarters

Ever willing to be distracted, one of the clients might ask Ninon to send for one of the Armenian seamstresses who was reputed to be very good at reading fortunes from coffee grounds. There were always a few women who succumbed to wishful thinking and chose something entirely unsuitable. In such cases Ninon, with admirable diplomacy, would tactfully direct them towards something likelier to flatter, though there were times when even she found it difficult, if not impossible, to deflect their attention from something they particularly fancied.

She had also opened a beauty salon with slimming treatments, installing what was then the latest equipment from Slenderella, quite popular then, but that was less of a success. So many ladies believed that a session on the slimming couch would remove all the effects of overindulgence that they were even less disciplined and careful about their diets than they had been before they came to the salon.

On that first visit, I was shown around, introduced to the team, and was eventually asked to try on some of the models that had already been made up. Preparing to model an outfit felt so wonderfully familiar in a place where nothing else so far had been. The concept of prêt-à-porter had yet to be adopted by top couture houses, and there was no large stock of ready-made clothes hanging on racks, either on view or in the back rooms. Ninon would purchase those designs from the Dior collection that she considered appropriate to her clientele and the climate. The patterns for the models she chose would be sent from Paris, and these, along with designated fabrics, trimmings, and accessories were all that was held in stock. After a client had settled on what she wanted and chosen a fabric from the swatches, Monsieur Pierre or Mademoiselle Laguy would swing into action, and the clothes would be made up to her measurements.

Ninon began using me as a model, sometimes when she wanted clothes shown in her own salons and at other times when she wanted a particular model seen and talked about; then as now, it was pretty much the same all over the world. I would wear an outfit to a big dinner party or other suitable occasion where it was sure to be noticed and return it to her the next day.

As the clientele became better acquainted with me, Ninon would sometimes send an urgent message when she herself was busy with a client and felt she could not neglect another equally important one who had arrived at the same time. I would receive a phone call asking me to be ready to hurry over in the car that was already on its way to me. She might be with a single lady or a group of them in one salon, and I would hurry to take over in the other one. I enjoyed the hours I spent at Pahlavi Avenue, where I felt I was making myself useful and was a genuine help to Ninon. It was a far cry from the hostility of the aunts and the tedium of idleness. I also entertained the secret hope that Queen Soraya might decide to pay a visit when I happened to be there. Alas, she never did.

***

My introduction to the shah's twin sister, Princess Ashraf, remains high on the list of many memorable 'firsts' during those early months. Ninon and Felix lived in a spacious two-storey villa on Ghazali Street, not far from the British and Soviet embassies. For the summer, the court, the smart set, and everybody else who could afford it would move to rented villas in Shemiran, if they did not already own one there. That summer, Ninon gave the first garden party of the season at the villa she had rented, with Princess Ashraf as the guest of honour. As the princess was known to be partial to asparagus, Ninon had some specially flown in from Europe on the morning of the party. It was only one of the many delicacies on the menu, but, afraid that her staff would make a complete botch of it, she had asked me to supervise its preparation and presentation.

When the princess's car drove up, I watched carefully to see how everybody behaved. The gentlemen bowed their heads about a third of the way down their chests and murmured 'Highness', and the ladies curtsied. When I was presented, I too curtsied, inclined my head and murmured 'Madame'.

After she had stopped to greet a few people, it was time to move to the dining room, where a sumptuous buffet had been laid out. Very few chairs had been placed along the walls, as guests were expected to stand in her presence. Princess Ashraf indicated that a chair was to be brought to the table for her, made herself comfortable, turned to scan the gathering, and crooked her finger when she spotted me, to indicate I should approach. She then ordered another chair to be brought for me, and thoroughly embarrassed at being singled out in this fashion, I sat down beside her. I should have been flattered, but at twenty-three, I felt pure nervousness in her presence, which was commanding and imperious. Her character, it was said, greatly resembled that of her iron-willed father.

I was quite relieved when the meal was over. An aide drew me aside later that evening and suggested that 'Highness' was a more suitable form of address than 'Madame'. I do not believe that the instruction came from the princess, as she never objected when I continued to address her as Madame, exactly as I would have done the sister of a French king. For all her fearsome reputation, Princess Ashraf was always very gracious to me in all the years I knew her.

***

How to describe Ninon? There was, of course, an element of hero worship in my admiration, which has not faded away in the fifty years since I first met her. She was brunette, with fine features and a trim figure; not very tall; always beautifully groomed; and turned out in perfect taste. The French phrase, *femme d'esprit*, catches that captivating blend of charm and animation that makes a woman who has those qualities, and uses them with intelligence, far more alluring than a beautiful face. Wit, tact, and discretion had ensured that Ninon retained His Majesty's friendship and was a regular guest at the palace, without giving rise to the idle gossip that inevitably accompanies the most trivial doings of those in the public eye.

During the course of their regular bridge sessions, the shah would occasionally ask Ninon and Felix for news of Zulu. 'So what's Zolqadr been up to now?'

It was HM's way of keeping track of Zulu, who was remembered not only as his instructor at the military academy but as somebody whose pranks and exploits used to be recounted at the family dinner table with amusement by his late father. When Princess Ashraf and I were better acquainted she told me that they used to ask their father to tell them what Ali Zolqadr had done that day. Once it was reported that, unable to find other transport, he had driven a tank into town to fetch some dancing girls to the barracks. There was not enough room inside the tank, so he drove through the streets of the city with the girls standing atop and waving animatedly to passers-by. He was demoted of course, but suffered no worse.

While I do not know whether Ninon and Felix had actually brought up the subject of Zulu's uncertain future after the operation on his chest and his obligatory retirement from the legion, they had certainly spoken up in his favour when the opportunity presented itself. It was to them and to HM's cousin Nasser Ali Pahlavan, who had shared the anxious hours of my vigil outside the operation theatre of Percy Hospital, and perhaps also to Queen Soraya's intervention on his behalf, that Zulu owed his reprieve and recall to Iran.

He had been reinstated with the rank of brigadier general, and had taken up his duties though I was not very clear as to what they were, as he was not based in one particular office and was not required to be in uniform. He had declared that he would wear no uniform other than that of the Foreign Legion, and whether it was out of courtesy to the legion[26] or to his personal preference, he was allowed to remain in mufti. In retrospect, it might have been appropriate to whatever role he was given.

***

Tehran boasted a lively social life. Zulu and I did not lack invitations, and for entertainment we would go to Le Colbey, a popular nightclub, or other fashionable spots where I would show off one of Ninon's models. We were having a thoroughly good time, but neither of us liked living with my in-laws.

The atmosphere in the house had begun to weigh on both of us. It was large enough to accommodate the six of us who occupied it, but there seemed no way of establishing a truce, if not a peace, between the aunts and myself. My father-in-law, though uninterested in the affairs of the women in his house, was not amiable on the rare occasions when he bothered to notice me. Zulu was away at work the whole day, and I had to bear the brunt of the sneering, sniggering, and petty intrigues of the aunts and the slovenly Zeenat, all determined to make my life as unpleasant as they could.

---

[26] One of HM's younger brothers, the late Prince Ali Reza, had served in the Foreign Legion.

Evidently they hoped that they could make me unhappy enough to provoke me into leaving Zulu and running back to France. My marriage to Elrikh had already taught me how to survive in an uncongenial environment, and I was determined not to be cowed by them.

Chapter 12

TEHRAN

1957-58

Over the centuries, invasions, migrations, and traffic along the maritime and overland trade routes to the country then known as Persia had brought settlers who contributed diversity to a population already quite varied in its ethnic and linguistic make-up. A large community of Armenians, mostly artisans, had been in the country for generations; after the 1917 Bolshevik Revolution, this was further enlarged by Russian-educated professionals, mainly Armenian and, to a lesser extent, Russian.

From well before this time, as a result of geography and constant contact, there already existed a considerable cultural affinity with Imperial Russia. Iran's first diplomatic contacts with the West had been with France, but the proximity of Russia to the north and the British to the east in India and their continual intervention in the affairs of the country had given rise to national preoccupations that overshadowed those early ties. By the beginning of the twentieth century, the

United States had been invited to reorganise the finances of the country, and several European countries were providing expertise in fields not already reserved for themselves by the British or the Russians.

When Reza Shah took power, his suspicion of the British and Russians led him to look elsewhere for technical expertise and advice for his ambitious projects, and contracts tended to be awarded to companies that were not British or Russian-owned.

Many Iranians who had studied abroad had returned as married men, and the result was an ethnic mix with a noticeably Western cultural slant among the affluent classes. In the early '50s, Iran began to emerge from an economic depression after its showdown over oil royalties with the British government and entered its boom period in the mid-'50s. There was heightened international interest in the country, now seen as the new El Dorado; the effect of this was to bring an even more varied spectrum of people to the country, all seeking fortune or fame and usually both.

So many projects were under way all over the country – dams, roads, and public buildings, all commissioned with the intention of transforming and modernising the country – that visitors could well have mistaken the entire country for an enormous building site.

This frenetic activity was in even greater evidence in Tehran, where the atmosphere of the city closely resembled that of a frontier town. New buildings, public and private, were going up everywhere; new townships were springing up like mushrooms; luxury goods and expensive cars were imported; and different nationalities could be encountered and a babel of languages heard. In tandem with public expenditure, private fortunes were being made at great speed and being spent with considerable extravagance. And there were parties galore.

Iranians are a hospitable and generous people and love entertaining; among the wealthy and the upper middle classes, there was easy social intermingling among the sexes. And since Reza Shah's time, there had been a far greater degree of freedom for women in Iran than in most Muslim countries of the region. Ours were the newest faces on an extremely active social scene, and those early months in Tehran were filled with invitations. I met a bewildering succession of people, most of whom had known Zulu in the past, and those who had not known him earlier could always wangle an introduction through somebody who knew somebody else. People were curious about his new wife, his youthful pranks had given him a certain notoriety, and his return had invited curiosity and gossip. Even without accepting every invitation that was pressed upon Zulu, we went to a seemingly unending series of receptions and parties.

I was beginning to gain some confidence with the advances I had made in learning Farsi, but I still had a lot to learn about the customs governing Iranian hospitality, which were quite outside anything in my experience. I discovered this to my great embarrassment when we were invited to the housewarming of a newly rich family. The house and what furnishings I could see as we were met in the foyer by our host displayed a lavishness that, to my European taste, bordered on the ostentatious, but a fine carpet covering most of the large entrance hall caught my eye as we came in, and I could not help exclaiming with pleasure, and complimenting our host on its beauty.

'*Pish-kesh*,' said our smiling host, as Zulu protested.

A lively exchange followed, and though I understood very little of what was being said, I was alarmed to realise that, in wanting to be polite and say something pleasant, I appeared to have committed a solecism and perhaps offended our host.

'What have I done now?' I asked Zulu as soon as we moved away.

Our host, he explained, felt obliged to offer me the carpet because I had admired it so enthusiastically; he, Zulu, had had to explain that I was newly arrived in Iran and unfamiliar with the customs of the country, and also to insist that there was no question of my accepting it. It was neither the expected, nor the polite, reply.

Clearly, it was going to take a bit longer for me to find my way safely through this minefield of courtesies, where a sincere and heartfelt compliment could place both the giver and the recipient of it under a heavy obligation.

I had a flashback to my early teens in Paris, when I had become friendly with a young Iranian student who, I now realised, was probably sent to France under the scholarship scheme established by Reza Shah and continued by his son. When I admired a handsome ring set with a turquoise that he wore, he took it off his finger and offered it to me, using the same expression, *'Pish-kesh'*, though I did not understand it. I was tempted and then disappointed when Maman made it plain that the offer was generous of him but to accept such an expensive gift was out of the question. I now understood that my young Iranian friend had reacted in a manner not at all unusual among his own people.

***

It was going to be necessary for me to learn as much as I could about Iran, and learn it fast. When I met Maryam, a friendly outgoing young woman of my age who was already a mother of four, I asked her to help me improve my spoken Farsi and teach me how to read it. I also asked her to accompany me to see films in order to help me understand the customs. We began lessons right away; sometimes we went to see a film, sometimes to the bazaar, and I would make a determined effort to read at least part of the newspaper or an article in a magazine every day. I felt I was making good progress in understanding and conversation, though deciphering the script was proving somewhat more frustrating.

Our lessons, but not our friendship, came to a stop when I left unexpectedly for a long visit to France. In later years, I have often wondered what became of her young sons when the country was at war in the '80s. They would then have been of just the right age to be sent out into the fields to trigger hidden mines ahead of the advancing troops, an inhumane and barbaric practice I thought.

At evening gatherings, perhaps after discussing politics or the latest news, there would often be recitals of poetry, which Persians love and of which they can quote verses. This too, along with the custom of offering pellets of opium, was a centuries-old tradition.

***

Nine months after we had been in Tehran, a mutual friend introduced a wealthy businessman to Zulu. The man's wife spoke very little French and needed a female companion to accompany her to Paris, where she had a series of medical consultations over a stay lasting some weeks. Our friend had brought him to meet Zulu, to find out whether I could accompany the wife. Such matters had to be settled between men, and it would have been quite incorrect of the man or his wife to approach me directly. It was, moreover, necessary to obtain Zulu's agreement as Iranian law did not allow a wife to leave the country without her husband's permission. We were delighted, as all my expenses would be paid, and the trip would give me a respite from my in-laws and a chance to see my parents and Taïssia, whom I missed terribly.

I might have wondered in passing whether my Farsi would be up to translating French medical terms, but I discovered on the flight to Paris that I need not have worried at all. The woman, a flighty social butterfly, had no intention of being chaperoned and had no need whatsoever of medical attention. The doctor was also her lover, and the 'medical consultation' was, in fact, a *rendezvous amoureux*. My Farsi was certainly good enough to understand that much, and the fact that she was counting on my discretion, of which I earnestly assured her. I was amused by the subterfuge and admiring of the ingenuity with which she had arranged her amorous escapade.

We parted company politely at the airport, where she made it clear that I was free to go directly to my parents' flat while she continued on to her hotel. Apart from a few telephone calls for form's sake, I had no news from her for the remainder of her stay. I stayed on in Paris after she left and have no idea what she told her husband when she returned to Tehran. As they were not part of our social circle, I did not have to meet them again and was spared the awkwardness of having to give the husband invented imaginary reports of our doings and his wife's medical condition.

***

I had spoken to my parents about the misery of living with my in-laws, reassuring them that I liked Iran nevertheless and wanted to go back. I explained that this time my reluctance to return had nothing to do with my husband and everything to do with his aunts and his father. Papa acted without hesitation; he rang Zulu and said that he would not agree to my returning to Iran until such time as Zulu could move us out of the family house and into independent accommodation. Zulu assured him it as already in hand.

***

When I returned to Tehran a few weeks later, I was met at the airport by Fathollah and was driven directly to a small building in a new area under development. We walked up a flight to a flat on the first floor. Decorated in blue and white, it had been furnished by him from the storerooms of the Crown properties. It was he, of course, who had found us the flat as well. Within walking distance of Nasser Ali Pahlavan's house a couple of streets away, the building was a new construction marooned like a beached boat, as it were, in an unpaved no-man's land of half-finished buildings.

These were temporary inconveniences of little consequence compared with the advantage I had gained – the hostile unfriendliness of my in-laws could no longer affect my daily life, and we had somewhere which we could call home.

Zulu and I had not occupied the flat for very long before we had guests who announced their arrival in an unexpected fashion. We heard rifle shots outside and many loud male voices; I turned to him for an explanation, but he did not know what these sounds signified any more than I did. When we went downstairs to investigate the commotion outside, we saw a dusty ramshackle Cadillac convertible parked on the uneven road in front of the entrance, disgorging an assortment of men dressed in the traditional shalwar kameez of rural Iran. They were waving rifles and firing shots in the air, but their manner was not at all aggressive or threatening.

Before he could explain their presence to me, they had all converged on Zulu. He was swamped in hearty embraces and backslapping, which took a few minutes, after which we were introduced. Zulu's Kurdish cousins had come to pay him a visit. When we invited them in, only the eldest, clearly their leader, came in with a much younger man who looked as if he could be his son; the other men were instructed to remain outside 'to guard us', Zulu told me with a straight face.

The only word to describe these visitors is *folklorique*, and I found it difficult to stifle my giggles. I knew the Zulgadars had family in the mountains, but nothing I had seen so far had prepared me for an encounter with a group of moustachioed men festooned with cartridge belts, who removed their shoes but kept their weapons when they came to make a friendly social call. While we arranged ourselves cross-legged on the carpet, I was careful not to catch Zulu's eye, as I knew I would not be able to keep from breaking out into loud laughter if I did.

As tea was brought in, the leader of the delegation said something to Zulu, smiling and inclining his head in my direction. He had noticed the Hermès scarf with its equestrian motifs around my neck and wanted to know whether horses had any special significance for me. Zulu explained that my father and uncle had both been Cossack officers and that I had a great affection for horses and loved riding. A broad smile lit up the cousin's face, and with a graceful gesture in my direction, he said, 'It is my honour to present your wife with a mare as a wedding gift.'

He then offered to look after her for as long it suited us.

I was struck by the strong and lasting tribal and family ties that had made them undertake the journey to wish us happiness and welcome me to the family and the unforced warmth with which they expressed themselves.

They left after Zulu promised to bring me to visit them, and I am sorry we never did. They sent word to let us know that the mare was carrying and again after she had dropped her foal safely. I suppose there is now a whole herd from that line which belongs to me, technically at least.

The gift of a horse was, under any circumstances, a generous one, but the full significance of this particular one came to me after they had left. Horses had been an integral part of the lives of these tribes for millennia. The stud farms of the Zagros, where these cousins lived, have existed and have been breeding fine stock since ancient times, even as far back as when the region had been subject to the Babylonian empire. Its prized horses constituted the principal tribute sent to the emperors. Zulu's own forefathers had been famous breeders of horses in the Caucasus, and this had been the source of their considerable wealth before oil was found in Azerbaijan. The same oil which had brought the country riches had also led to the loss of everything they had, making Zulu rootless and homeless for most of his life. This was the tribe's way of welcoming me into the family and helping him to a fresh start. A young wife and a brood mare would give him the children and the horses, which, for them, were the primary sources of happiness and wealth.

I felt we had been shown a special mark of esteem when we discovered that they had made the journey for the sole purpose of meeting us and were not planning to call on my father-in-law. We did not mention the visit to him, but he was quite offended when, as was inevitable, somebody gossiped and he learnt of it. The visit of those fierce-looking mountain men, their dignity and spontaneous warmth, is one of the happiest memories of my years in Iran.

***

I was less enchanted by another member of the family – Zulu's brother, Rashid. An engineer, and the eldest of the three siblings, he had recently come to Iran, where he was employed by a company involved in the construction of the Karaj dam in the Alborz mountains. This huge project, which was not far from Tehran, had been awarded to an American firm, and though Rashid had not lived in Iran for many years, he spoke Farsi and knew his way around. That, no doubt, was the reason he had been chosen for the post. He had completed his studies in Germany before the war, married a German girl, and settled there.

The Fourth Wife of Aliyar Bey

The Allied forces had imprisoned him for his wartime activities when they entered Germany. Nobody would tell me what exactly he had done, except that it was thanks to Zulu, who was also in Germany at that time and had interceded on his behalf, that he was released. There was no love lost between the brothers, but he was family, and Zulu had been duty-bound to come to his aid; I already had a recent example of how Iranians respected and honoured those bonds.

I had not met Rashid earlier because he had never made the journey from Germany to France to visit Zulu in hospital, and I could not help but compare his ingratitude and lack of concern for his wounded brother with that of their Kurdish cousins, with whom Zulu seemed to have more in common. Physically too, I found the brothers quite different. Rashid tended towards corpulence and did not have their father's, or Zulu's, presence or military bearing. Knowing what I did about him, perhaps I was prejudiced against him and disliked him, and the feeling was probably mutual.

It was at a party hosted by Rashid, attended by the usual mix of diplomats, businessmen, and people connected with the dam project, that Zulu averted what could have turned into an embarrassing diplomatic incident. He overheard a conversation between a secretary from the French embassy and an Iranian guest, though, as he later told me, it was a pretty one-sided conversation. The woman was haranguing the poor man, wanting to know why Iran was not supporting the Algerians, fellow Muslims after all, in their fight for independence. The man might well have wondered why a Frenchwoman should be expressing views so unsympathetic to her country. Apart from that, her behaviour was ill-advised and improper in every way, and a blatant abuse of her diplomatic immunity – as an official, however minor, representing her country, as a guest in Iran, and not least because it could have got the Iranian into serious trouble. Wisely but in vain, the man had tried to steer her away from the subject and restricted himself to mumbling a few innocuous phrases when she persisted.

Zulu arranged for her to be invited to another, much smaller, party a few days later, when it was not difficult to bring the talk around to what seemed to be her pet subject. Her conversation took the same turn as before; a recording of her conversation had been organised and there were now witnesses as well, it was sufficient evidence of her indiscretion, so it needed no more than a word in the right quarters to arrange for her recall. Though we never found out whether it affected her subsequent career, I was sure Zulu had made an enemy for life – not that it was of the slightest concern to him. Her superiors could not have been aware of her views, but once these came to their knowledge, they could not overlook her lack of diplomacy and of judgment. She can hardly have been ignorant of the fact that Iran was not a country in which to express such opinions. While her government might do no more than slap her on the wrist, an Iranian might suffer much worse at the hands of his. It was the first time I had an inkling of Zulu's influence behind the scenes.

Chapter 13

Queen and Shahbanou

In 1953, a few years before we came to Iran, the shah and his prime minister of the time, Dr Mossadegh, had disagreed over Iran's oil policy. This resulted in serious consequences for HM, for Dr Mossadegh, and for the country. Dr Mossadegh, confident of his popularity, led an attempt to oust the shah. Their Majesties were obliged to leave the country and fled to Italy. They waited there for some days while General Fazlollah Zahedi, an old ally of Reza Shah, took charge of the situation and restored order. Dr Mossadegh had completely misjudged the level of support in favour of the monarchy; public opinion had swiftly swung back in favour of the shah, and the royal couple was able to return to Iran after a few days. General Zahedi replaced Dr Mossadegh as prime minister.

Apart from ambitious politicians making a bid for more power, no shortage of radicals abounded, malcontents, and religious leaders who, at various times, railed against the monarchy and tried to whip up sufficient public enthusiasm to call for its abolition. For the majority of the population, however, it was still unthinkable to be governed by committee and not ruled by a king. Whatever Iran's tribal and regional divisions, however distant and unapproachable the representatives of the monarchy might be, the institution itself was still deeply rooted in the consciousness and culture of the people. By the time we arrived in 1956, the shah was, to all appearances, popular and firmly in control.

There was, however, no male heir to the throne, and wherever I went, it was a subject for endless discussion. His Majesty's first consort, Queen Fawzia, had given him a daughter, Princess Shahnaz. The princess was now in her teens and newly married to General Zahedi's son. His second wife, Queen Soraya, was childless after six years of marriage; His Majesty's younger brother, Prince Ali Reza, had been crown prince until his death in a plane crash in 1954. The ever-present threat of assassination loomed over the Shah, and without a male heir, there could be no coronation until one was born. All this had placed great pressure on the shah to assure the succession. Rumour and gossip about His Majesty's intentions in this regard were not confined to the ladies passing an idle afternoon in Ninon's salons.

The fairy-tale aura and romance surrounding the royal couple had provided plenty of material over the years for the international press. Their preoccupations and troubles were grist to the mill of every newspaper and magazine; every little detail and snippet that could be gleaned from any source was reported and dissected with relish. The queen was barren, and her frantic and frequent visits to consult specialists in Europe were no longer a secret from the world. She found it humiliating, and in growing anguish she had become withdrawn and rarely appeared in public. It now remained to be seen whether the shah would divorce her in order to marry again, or whether, as was permitted by Islam, he would take another wife. In the event of his doing so, and in the event of that wife producing a male heir, Queen Soraya would, of course, be supplanted, if not in the shah's affections, then in position and importance.

Nevertheless she was still obliged to continue with her queenly duties, and a rare occasion was when she invited a group of local designers to present their own creations at a specially organised fashion show to be held at Golestan Palace, using silks from Yazd, muslins and chiffons from Chaluz, and brocades designed by the School of Fine Arts in Tehran. The intention was to showcase traditional Iranian textiles in a modern context. The queen was patroness of the event, which was to be held in the banquet hall of Golestan Palace. Ninon's workshops hummed with activity, and I was busy with fittings and rehearsals.

At Golestan Palace, the only convenient room that could be used by the models as a dressing room was some way down a corridor that ran along the rear of the banquet hall. All the other designers were presenting one outfit each, but Monsieur Pierre and Mademoiselle Laguy were so thrilled to be invited to create something of their own, that they had, in their enthusiasm, produced nine ensembles. It was expected that Ninon would choose one or two, but she decided to show all nine. It meant a breathless dash between changes along the corridor for me, her only model. The pièce de résistance of the show, which is always presented last, was one of Monsieur Pierre and Mademoiselle Laguy's creations – an evening dress in midnight blue brocade.

Ninon had come in to supervise us and make sure that not even the smallest detail had been overlooked while I was getting ready. The two of us walked towards the banquet hall, and as we approached, the attendants opened the side door we were using to let us enter, or so we thought. It was, in fact, to let the queen slip out discreetly. Intent on doing a last-minute inspection before I entered, I was looking down to check my dress and walked straight into her.

Ninon started presenting excuses on our behalf just as I looked up, recognised the famous green eyes, and started stammering in nervous embarrassment. The queen said she was leaving because she thought the show was over but praised the brocade dress before continuing on her way out; in spite of my confusion, I had the wits to notice and admire the celadon green suit and matching pillbox hat she wore, which enhanced the colour of her eyes. Queen Soraya's star may have been on the wane, but she was, without any doubt, still the most glamorous woman in Iran.

***

She left Iran not long after that and never returned. Ninon's seventeen-year-old daughter, Manon, was at school in Switzerland and rang her mother to say, 'Maman, Soraya isn't coming back to Iran! I've just heard it on the Swiss radio. She says she has been repudiated! Is it true?'

It was the first we had heard of such a thing, as an official announcement had yet to be made in Iran. The rest of Queen Soraya's life was spent in search of something – satisfaction, happiness, serenity, an attachment to replace the one that was denied her? She is long gone now, but for my generation, she was an iconic figure whose magic was not dimmed with the loss of her position or her title.

Queen Soraya's departure was followed by a period of hectic social activity at court.

It was known how deeply the shah had been affected by the divorce. To those of us on the sidelines, it seemed that the frenzied partying was an escape and a denial rather than the reaction of somebody freed from unwelcome restraint.

Ninon had asked me to stop by at her salon to give her a hand with some task; on arrival, I was directed to the patio, where she was deep in discussion with a visitor from the palace, a man I recognised vaguely as a crony of His Majesty. She waved to me to join them there. They were going over a guest list together, and she looked up from it to say, 'I expect you have already met Khanum-e-Zolqadr[27]?'

He gave me a look that was both appraising and dismissive, and it made me squirm with distaste. Later that day an invitation was delivered to our flat, requesting my presence at a 'small soirée' at the palace the next evening. Zulu was away on a hunting

---

[27] A title of respect while referring to or addressing, a lady

trip, and I had no way of getting word to him in time; naively, I believed that it gave me sufficient excuse to decline. Not so, Ninon informed me; barring illness, I could not refuse. She dismissed my wardrobe as inadequate and ordered a cocktail dress made up immediately. I was her cousin's wife and needed to be suitably dressed to uphold the honour of the family.

I had never attended any of these parties alone and was not looking forward to it as I returned home late the next afternoon with a slinky black lace dress straight out of Ninon's workshop. Zulu had walked in just before I got home, and I was relieved to be able to ring Ninon to tell her that he had just returned and was not feeling very well. I begged her to make suitable apologies, which she must have done, and no further mention was made of the occasion, not to either of us, at least.

It seemed HM was ready to marry again, and his name was linked in the international press with a number of titled ladies and famous beauties. In the meantime, in Tehran, the feverish manoeuvring among the well-connected to sponsor a suitable candidate was embarrassing to observe, it was, after all for the most exalted position to which any young woman in the country could aspire. These matters are traditionally handled by older women, and clearly a lot of goodwill was being tapped, past favours were being called in, and future debts were being incurred in an effort to present a daughter, a protégée, a favourite niece, or a young cousin for vetting and approval by the royal ladies. No hopeful was likely to be in the running without facing and overcoming that first hurdle. Some mothers had gone to the extent of taking their daughters to Paris to be photographed by the best portrait photographers there. They would bring the photographs to Ninon, asking her to intercede on their behalf. All this was quite alien to me, apart from which I found it rather tasteless and undignified.

Once the announcement of the shah's engagement to Miss Farah Diba was made, it was not long before Ninon's workshops resembled a series of caves full of industrious dwarves, the Armenian embroidery women in their room, the seamstresses in another, Monsieur Pierre gesturing around his perfectly structured suits, and Mademoiselle fluttering about her flowing confections. We did not have long to put together and present an entire trousseau, and it required a lot of coordination; accessories and furs had to be sourced to match the clothes, not to mention the jewellery, which would come from Harry Winston. The whole collection would be presented by Ninon at a private viewing. During the course of these preparations, we made a new friend.

Freddy Horowitz was based in Harry Winston's Geneva office and made several visits to Tehran while we were getting ready for the presentation. Our flat became a second home where he could relax, speak Russian, and be free of the protocol and formality required at the palace. He and Zulu always had much to discuss concerning the complicated security arrangements that had been made for the transport and safekeeping of the jewels. I was not the one getting married, but between fittings for the show and trying on jewellery, it certainly felt like it!

The creation of an entire collection for the trousseau had been Princess Ashraf's idea, and the first presentation took place at her palace. Apart from the two models, an Italian flown in especially for the occasion, and myself, only three people were present in the long gallery-like room – the princess, the future queen[28], and Ninon. They sat at the far end, the princess and Miss Diba on a sofa, and Ninon in an armchair by them, making notes as they watched us walking the length of the room to approach them. Ninon would place a tick against her list when they approved of something, after which that particular model would no longer be available to anybody else.

Princess Ashraf beckoned me over as the three of them were discussing a closely fitted black cocktail dress that Miss Diba admired but that she thought might be too snug on her. The princess was explaining that, as the Dior representative, Ninon's couture house held the design and could make it up to her size. Court protocol required Ninon to take any dress ordered by the future queen out of circulation and the paper pattern destroyed so it could not be used again, but on this occasion, permission had been granted for the entire collection, including the clothes chosen by Miss Diba, to be worn for the two further shows for which invitations had already been sent. They then asked to see the heavy bracelet on my wrist and a large diamond-studded hairpin that held my chignon.

---

[28] The title of Shahbanou was had been devised specifically for Empress Farah and had come into use after the coronation in 1967. Prior to this, queens were addressed as Malika.

The Fourth Wife of Aliyar Bey

'Hélène-jaan, let us have a closer look at that pin you've got in your hair.'

I stood in front of them while Miss Diba looked slightly surprised at the familiarity with which Princess Ashraf spoke to me.

'Don't worry. She's part of the family. She's the wife of Ninon's cousin, Ali,' the princess said carelessly.

I removed the pin and left it on the coffee table in front of them, and as I turned to walk back with wisps of hair falling around my face, I saw the princess pick up the pin and pop it into the future queen's handbag, saying, 'This is your engagement present, my dear.'

'Where's the diamond hairpin?' Freddy asked me in consternation when I came into the changing room. He did not know whether to be horrified at such casual treatment of an extremely expensive piece of jewellery or pleased that things had gotten off to such a promising start.

The two further presentations of the collection, took place at Ninon's salons in Pahlavi Avenue. The ladies of the privileged inner circle had been invited along with their husbands, the latter having received a discreet reminder to keep their chequebooks handy. Zulu was handling the security for these two occasions as well. Armed guards and plainclothesmen were posted inside and all around the building. There were so many small jewelled accessories to complement the clothes, we even had them standing over us as we pinned on a brooch or slid on a jewelled hairpin.

Of all the jewellery in that collection, I particularly admired and was thrilled to be the one allowed to show a magnificent emerald and diamond necklace and another one consisting of three cascading rows of sumptuously large pearls. I promised Freddy Horowitz that the pearls would cause a stir but refused to give him any further details. When he kept on badgering me, Ninon just laughed and told him to have a little more faith in us instead of becoming so anxious.

There was a swirling high-collared coat in silver-gray mink, with deep patch pockets, which we had decided to show over a clinging strapless black velvet dress trimmed in white feathers across the bust. Apart from the pearls around my neck, I wore no jewellery. I swished through the two salons with the coat buttoned right up to the neck, and my hands tucked out of sight in the pockets, giving people time to admire its styling and the rich sheen of the fur. I then unbuttoned it and strolled slowly through the salons a second time, bare-shouldered, trailing the mink behind me, relishing the indrawn breaths of admiration as the size and glow of the pearls were seen to full advantage over the black and white dress.

'How much for the pearls?' one guest whispered as I paused.

I whispered the figure that had been mentioned and watched her eyes grow round as I murmured it before slinking on. It was more than a princely sum; it was a king's ransom.

It would have been lèse-majesté for anybody to aspire to the emerald and diamond necklace, or the pearls; they were, without a doubt, destined to be displayed on a royal neck, and it was no surprise that they went to the Crown. But it was a fine collection with many other beautiful, if smaller, pieces, all shown in ideal conditions to a carefully selected gathering. The husbands and the chequebooks did not stand a chance.

The whole affair had been a great success, Freddy Horowitz was discreetly triumphant, and I had loved every minute of it.

Chapter 14

LE BISTROT

Tehran 1959

Television was still in its infancy, so the royal wedding was not televised in Iran.

I had nothing against which to compare it, but my recollection of it is that, though it was attended by elaborate protocol and security measures and was on a somewhat grander scale, it was not very different from a marriage in a rich and important family. Newspapers carried photographs and reports, notables and envoys were present, the city celebrated as befitted the occasion, but it should be remembered that it was the third of its kind. Whatever rejoicing there was on that day was nothing to the jubilation that would come with the birth of a son and heir. When the fervent prayers of a nation were answered would be the time for the real celebrations.

***

The Fourth Wife of Aliyar Bey

Our own preoccupations also had to do with children. We had spent an evening with Nazem, who was now comfortably installed with an attractive companion in a beautiful house. He had a good cook and threw wonderful parties. At this particular one, we met an American couple who were newly arrived in Tehran – Henry Stephen, press attaché at the US embassy, and his wife, Karin. He was a photographer, and she had spent her childhood and early life in China and South Africa. They were friendly and outgoing, and we had taken an immediate liking to them.

We met often after that evening, and playing with their lovable two-year-old daughter Pindie, made me long to have Taïssia with us. We had already been in Iran for three years, knew plenty of people, had a full social calendar, and were happy together. But we were financially stretched.

Elrikh had been so irregular with his child support payments that we were obliged to send money to my parents to meet Taïssia's expenses. Anyway, they were getting too old to manage a child of her age, and I felt it was high time for her to come and live with us. Much as I liked helping out at Ninon's, which gave me an opportunity to spend time with the smart set and to wear a lot of beautiful clothes that weren't mine, it brought no material rewards. I was twenty-six, and we both hoped there would be more children. A high-ranking Iranian army officer's pay was not enough to meet our own expenses, let alone allow us to bring up a family in comfort. We came to the conclusion that Zulu would either have to find another means of supplementing his salary or look for another job.

He decided to resign from the army. There remained the delicate matter of how to inform His Majesty. Once more, we turned to Fathollah and to Zulu's immediate superior, General Bahram Ariana, for advice on how to go about it without appearing ungrateful. Together, they decided that the letter should be written in French, a language with which the shah was entirely at ease and in which Zulu felt he was able to express himself with the appropriate formality, better than he might have done in Farsi.

'Sire,' Zulu wrote, expressing gratitude and emphasising how conscious he was of HM's generosity towards him but humbly requesting now that he be permitted to leave the army in order to seek a means of better supporting himself and his family. We awaited the answer nervously.

The world did not fall about our heads, and His Majesty is reported to have read the letter and said quite mildly, 'Zolqadr can go off and find another job if he wants, but he should remember that, as far as I am concerned, he has left neither the army nor my service.'

Perhaps it had been Fathi himself who had put forward the idea to His Majesty, but at any rate, it was he who was instructed to come up with a suitable alternative for Aliyar. The project he found for us was ideal, as it would allow both of us to work together.

The Hotel Caspien was one of the better hotels in Tehran, though that was not saying much. It had a badly run restaurant, Le Bistrot. We were being offered a chance to take over Le Bistrot and bring it up to international standards, a job the owner was happy to leave to somebody else. I am not of an idle nature, and Aliyar, with his sociable and expansive personality, liked the idea of having a free hand with it, so we were enthusiastic about the idea, and promptly said, 'Yes thank you, when can we start?'

The hotel itself was an uninteresting barracks-like six-storey building on Takht-e-Jamshid Avenue, somewhat north of the city centre. Whatever Tehran's hopes and aspirations for the future, many of its streets were still no better than dirt tracks.

Takht-e-Jamshid Avenue was one of the first to be asphalted over. It had become fashionable for the affluent, who had hitherto lived close to the palaces and administrative buildings in the lower-lying centre of the city, to move to cooler and higher ground north in the foothills of the Alborz mountains, where summer residences were being transformed for year-round use. The city itself was expanding so rapidly that, shortly after we took over the restaurant, the areas surrounding the hotel had been built up, and the location was considered quite central. The newly opened shops along it were ample proof of this, doing very well selling souvenirs to tourists of the sort who would not go off the beaten path for their purchases. The buildings themselves were rarely of any architectural interest, but they were new and they were 'modern' and that was all that was required.

American-style chains like the Hilton or the Intercontinental had not yet come to Tehran, and as the Hotel Caspien was not far from the American embassy, it catered to a largely expatriate, and largely American, clientele. The Americans were filling the gap left by the British, who were further resented after their occupation of Iran in the '40s, the fracas over oil royalties, and the subsequent British blockade of Iran in the '50s. Among the guests at the Caspien, one might find technicians and advisors of every kind, resident in the hotel while in Iran on short postings, or parked there with their families while waiting to move into longer term accommodation.

Restaurant was a complete misnomer for Le Bistrot, which was a rather seedy snack bar. We were able to convince the owner that the outdated equipment in the basement kitchen would have to be replaced with modern fittings, without which, we insisted, it would not meet international standards of hygiene or be capable of producing the range and quality of cuisine with which we all hoped to attract a better class of clientele. But it was not a persuasive enough argument when it came to spending more money to renovate the dreary red and white interior of the 'restaurant', so we had to make do with strategically placed bowls of flowers.

The cuisine of old Persia is both varied and tasty, with influences from the surrounding countries, so our Iranian clientele would not be lacking in discernment, even if they were unfamiliar with Western dishes. We could not, however, be expected to cover every expectation of our foreign clientele. As we were working with untried staff, we decided to play it safe and offer a simple menu of French and international dishes that we ourselves knew how to cook and did not require complicated training and preparation. This would, we hoped, minimise the risk of disasters in the kitchen and during the service. Tehran is well supplied with fresh produce all year round, from the fertile shores of the Caspian during the warmer months and from the south in the winter. Though no restriction was placed on foreign imports, it was both wiser and more economical to rely as much as possible on local suppliers.

Le Bistrot was open for business.

We were not running the most fashionable restaurant in Tehran, but neither did we have much competition; it soon became quite popular with the expatriate set. Our cautious beginning and hard work began to pay off, and we felt confident enough to bring Taïssia to live with us.

Shortly after she arrived, a large group of our friends from the French embassy gave a farewell dinner at Le Bistrot for a colleague who was returning to France later that night. As we could not leave the running of the restaurant to the staff and spend the whole evening with our friends, we had offered to see off the departing diplomat at the airport after dinner was over. We had stopped at their table to chat with them for a few minutes during a lull in the service.

Suddenly, the floor seemed to ripple and the walls were shaking. Cutlery and plates came sliding off the tables and onto the floor with a crash. Zulu shouted, 'It's an earthquake,' and told us to remain seated with our backs to the walls while he went off to deal with the other guests, the kitchen, and the general pandemonium. Abolfas, our maître d'hôtel, was yelling something at me that I, in my fright, could not understand. It seemed everybody was running around shouting, but at least they knew what was happening and what to do – we foreigners did not.

Adrienne, one of the embassy wives, suddenly panicked when she remembered that she had given her three children and Taïssia, who was staying over with them that night, permission to sleep on the roof terrace – not the safest place to be at such a time. Zulu dashed off in the car to make sure that they were all right, telling us that under no circumstances were we to move out.

For the rest of that terrifying hour we sat there waiting for him to come back. He came back with the news that the children were safe, and when we finally left for the airport amid a few slight tremors, confused and frightened guests were still milling about the lobby of the hotel, some of them in their nightclothes.

Perhaps it was a wife's misplaced faith, but I was convinced Zulu was the best person to deal with an emergency, so I was relieved that it was he, and not the chauffeur, who would be driving. We ha no way of foretelling the condition of the road to the airport, and even if it was driveable, the fear of finding that the runway had been damaged and flights grounded was very real.

We did get to the airport, the runway was intact, and the flight was expected to take off with a minor delay. We even had time for a well-deserved drink, so we went into the deserted bar and placed our orders while waiting for the flight to be announced. The barman refused any payment when Zulu took out his wallet and said that, as everybody else had fled without settling up, there was no reason why the one honest customer of the evening should be the only one to pay.

The epicentre of the quake was a 100 kilometres away in Qazvin, but we learnt the next day that many hotel guests on the top floor who were already in their beds had been thrown onto the floor when the first shocks hit. That was my first experience of an earthquake. They are a common occurrence in Iran, and I had to learn to take them in my stride but never managed to overcome my terror of them.

***

I had stopped to talk to guests who sat at a table near the door when two men walked in one evening. I immediately recognised the one in front, who stopped dead in his tracks when he saw me. I was equally surprised but recovered my wits first, excused myself, and went towards them, calling out to him in Russian, 'You filthy aristocrat, what are you doing here?'

'I could ask you the same question,' retorted Boris, a fellow mischief-maker when, as children, we had both been in the same Russian playgroups and scout troops.

'It's my restaurant, you silly man,' I told him as he gathered me into a bear hug.

His soberly dressed companion watched with barely concealed embarrassment. Zulu had heard the commotion and emerged from somewhere to see his wife in the arms of an attractive man and asked loudly, 'Who's this?'

'Prince Boris Galitsine, my husband, Aliyar Zulgadar.'

Boris was travelling with a French businessman, who was bewildered by this extravagant and excessive Russian bonhomie but was obviously relieved when we were introduced and he discovered that his titled associate had not been embracing a mere waitress. They were on a business trip to Iran and its neighbouring countries, with Boris acting as guide and interpreter for the other man, who spoke nothing but French. Though Boris spoke neither Farsi nor Arabic, he did speak English; he had, moreover, savoir-faire, breeding, and a title.

Like most Russians of noble birth, he had grown up speaking French in preference to Russian and had a marked French accent when he spoke Russian. For many 'filthy aristocrats' on the run during the 1917 Revolution, the characteristic inability of native French speakers to pronounce an 'r' without rolling it in the Russian manner had been the fatal giveaway. When we were children, most of us, of less exalted lineage and therefore able to pronounce our 'r' as it should be in Russian, had teased him about his accent. Like others whose families had lost their wealth in that revolution, Boris had had to live by his wits, and apart from being very pleased to see him, I was glad that he seemed to be getting by with reasonable success.

One September, the only month when the golden caviar of the type known as 'imperial', is available. It is reserved for the royal family, hence the nomenclature. Zulu received a call from Jean Naville, a banker. Jean booked a table for the following evening and explained that his dinner guests were to be the journalist and writer Joseph Kessel and his Irish wife, Michèle. Zulu was looking very smug as he asked me to bring a large soup ladle over from the flat but would not tell me why. Neither had he told Jean Naville that he and Joseph Kessel, whom he referred to as Jeff, were old friends.

Kessel was fifteen years older than Zulu, and they had first met in Paris when Zulu was still an adolescent. Jeff was something of a prodigy at a young age, decorated for his role in the First World War, with a growing reputation as a journalist. The two men had much in common; they had both lived in several different countries while still very young, and both spoke several languages though Russian was the language spoken in their families. They moved easily between different circles and different cultures, and both had a similar appetite for adventure.

Jeff's parents were Lithuanian Jews who had settled in Argentina, where he was born. The family left Argentina when Jeff's father, Dr Kessel, took up a position in Orenburg, in the Urals, and lived there for some years before moving to France, where Dr Kessel had been a medical student. Jeff joined up during the First World War, first as a stretcher-bearer and then in the air force. Just twenty years old when the war ended, he was awarded a military medal for bravery, as well as the Military Cross.

He wrote for the most highly regarded French newspapers, managing to combine successfully his job as a reporter with his desire to travel and to assist at the great events of his time – the revolution in Ireland, the formation of Israel, the first commercial trans-Saharan flights. In the Second World War, he was a war correspondent before joining the Resistance and then escaping to England to join the Free French. With his nephew, the, writer Maurice Druon, he wrote *Le Partisan* which was to become the signature song of the French Resistance. At the end of that war, he received more decorations for bravery. To cap it all, they were followed by the Légion d'Honneur and then the highest recognition of literary merit in France; he was elected to the Académie Française.

After I had arrived at the restaurant with the ladle on the appointed evening, Zulu ordered me out of the kitchen with

The Fourth Wife of Aliyar Bey

instructions to send for him immediately when Jean Naville and his guests arrived early. It was an excuse to make sure I did not see the preparations. Jeff was duly delighted and surprised when Zulu emerged from the kitchen to greet them, and Jean duly entertained when he discovered that he was responsible for reuniting two old friends. In Jeff's honour, I was to join them, as Zulu could not leave the kitchen or restaurant unattended. He told Jean not to bother ordering a first course, which he had already arranged, compliments of the house.

Abolfas brought out an enormous bowl with the handle of the soup ladle sticking out of it. When he set it down in front of us, we saw it held a slightly smaller bowl, nestling in shaved ice and filled to the brim with golden caviar. Ladlesful of that, with lashings of vodka, made a very filling first course, with little room left over for anything else. It was a gesture typical of Zulu, but golden caviar was not for the general, and I wondered what promises he had been obliged to make, and to whom, to get a whole kilo of it. I also wondered how to restore the polish to a blackened silver soup ladle.

The Kessels were using Tehran as a base while Jeff was in and out of Afghanistan, researching the book, which would eventually be published under the title *The Horsemen*, and we would see quite a lot of them over the next few years.

I came to understand that, apart from the evident admiration each man had for the other, each envied the other's exploits. Each one, it seemed, wished he had been born earlier or later in order to have done what the other had. They might be brothers in spirit, but when Jeff broached the subject of a biography to Zulu, the answer was quite firm, 'Not in my lifetime.'

Jeff would regale me with tales of glittering receptions at the Zulgadars' house on Avenue Henri Martin. He described Zulu, a precocious teenaged charmer in a dinner jacket with a mischievous gleam in his eye, enjoying the attention he was getting from the women but bored with having to behave like an adult.

> 'He's still like that, isn't he?' he would ask me, and I would laughingly agree. I should have paid more heed to those words, insightful as they proved to be. Kessel died in 1979, leaving a body of work comprising some eighty books.

***

Our time at Le Bistrot came to an end two and a half years later, when Zulu had a disagreement with the proprietor of the hotel. It was ostensibly over the terms of our contract with him, but I suspect it was quite simply a question of greed – the restaurant had begun to do well, and the owner thought it would be easy enough to take over and run it by himself. If he believed he could maintain the standards we had set and continue to attract the same clientele, good luck to him, we said to each other when we left, angry rather than downcast by the abrupt end to this venture. We knew that, even with effort and imagination, he lacked the two ingredients that had made the difference between success and limping along – Aliyar's overwhelming presence and the encouragement we had received from a growing circle of friends and loyal clients. There was room enough in the expanding city for many more restaurants like Le Bistrot, and both of us were confident that something else was sure to come our way.

Chapter 15

SOUTHERN INTERLUDE

Isfahan, with its fine examples of Islamic architecture, its mosques and monuments, lies 350 kilometres from Tehran, on the way south to Shiraz and the waters of the Persian Gulf. Isfahan is an oasis in an otherwise arid region, it stands on a crossroads of a trading route that had been a halt for caravans and became, consequently, a busy trading centre since ancient times. Sixteenth-century European travellers to the city wrote with admiration of its splendid buildings, the religious tolerance enjoyed by its population, and the brilliance of the court of the Safavid rulers who had made it their capital. Isfahan lost its pre-eminence after it was besieged in the early eighteenth century; on their accession to power, the Qajar kings shifted the capital to Tehran at the end of the eighteenth century. But the beauty of the city, the enormous Naqsh-i-Jahan square with its domed blue mosque and its decoration of intricately patterned tiles that characterise the buildings of that period, continues to attract visitors and pilgrims into modern times.

The Fourth Wife of Aliyar Bey

The lands south of Isfahan and east of Ahvaz, a city on the Iran-Iraq border, are the home of the Bakhtiari[29], a federation of tribes, of whom a large number have remained pastoral nomads. Twice a year, with their herds and flocks, the Bakhtiari undertake an impressive and gruelling annual migration lasting upwards of four weeks as they move between their high summer pastures and winter quarters on lower lands. The Bakhtiari family, hereditary khans of one of the two main branches of the tribes, had played a prominent role in government and politics before Reza Shah's rise to power and had been a major factor in forcing the abdication of Mohammad Ali Shah Qajar in 1909.

In the 1930s, when Reza Shah began his crackdown on the autonomy of tribal chieftains, the Bakhtiari khans had been slow to yield to the authority of the state and had, in fact, been exceptionally troublesome. For this unruliness and flouting of authority, they were forbidden by Reza Shah to own or carry arms and were regarded with suspicion for the rest of his reign.

The situation was further exacerbated by the fact that Isfahan had a large German population. Inevitably, the majority of them came under suspicion as Europe prepared once more for war in the 1930s and carried over its quarrels into Iran. Soraya Esfandiari Bakhtiari, the daughter of Khalil Khan Bakhtiari and his German wife, was born in Isfahan in 1933 and spent her early years there. It was not until 1951, after she married Mohammed Reza Shah, that members of her family were sufficiently trusted by the shah to be appointed to sensitive

---

[29] Also referred to as 'Bakhtiar'

positions. Many continued to hold those positions and served the Crown faithfully even after Soraya left Iran following her divorce from Mohamed Reza Shah.

One of her cousins, Majid Bakhtiar, had entered politics and became a senator. His brother, Jamshid, invited us to visit him on his farm near Ahvaz. As the youngest in the family, Jamshid had been given the least productive of the family's holdings but was eager to show Aliyar what he was doing on the land. Aliyar had known the family since the 1930s, and Jamshid told me that he and his brothers had been in awe of Aliyar, who would be carrying out inspection trips, and was consequently the only man permitted to be fully armed whenever he visited them. The boys looked forward to his visits, because he would take them outside and discreetly teach them how to shoot; it was quite illegal to do so of course because, not only were they forbidden to possess firearms, even handling them was not allowed. Aliyar knew how much these young boys smarted under that restriction, and no doubt he also thought back to the uncertainty of his own life. He believed that boys in their situation ought to learn how to handle guns safely; he had shown them trust and respect, and they remembered this warmly even after they were grown men.

Jamshid's farm lay above a river and looked quite unpromising on that first visit. He had installed pumps to draw up water for irrigation and was adapting agricultural methods from all over the world to transform it slowly it into what was later recognised as a model farm. He grew wheat, the market garden yielded peas, but his pride and prize crop was globe artichokes. Aware that there was growing demand for exotic produce in Tehran, Jamshid had imported and planted a succulent variety of artichoke from Brittany. His Majesty was very partial to these, and following Aliyar's advice, Jamshid sent him a basketful when he brought in his first crop.

During our stay, a farmhand came with the news that the mechanic would have to be called to fix Mr Massey, who had developed an ailment. Apparently, the Arab labour referred to the two tractors as 'Mr Massey' and 'Mrs Ferguson'.

I was treated to an astonishing experience while we sat outdoors one evening; oil would seep upwards from the ground to form pools on the surface. The farmhands were instructed to set alight one of these pools so that a column of fire rose up from the earth. I had already heard of this, but the reality was an eerie sight and must have been effective and frightening when it had been used in warfare in ancient times.

Wild boar abounded in the area, breeding undisturbed, as they were shunned for food by the locals. When the men in our party shot one, the staff set it up on a spit to roast slowly for a convivial dinner under the stars. Upper-class Iranians, particularly those educated in the West, did not adhere as strictly to the religious restriction on eating pork as was the case among the more traditional middle and working classes.

There were, of course, no dietary constraints on me. Aliyar was nominally a Muslim, but I had never seen him show the slightest interest in religious observances or, indeed, in anything connected with religion. This lack of religious fervour had not gone against him under Reza Shah, even though His Majesty was a staunch Muslim himself.

On the contrary, his lack of religious observance or fervour had resulted in Aliyar's being chosen in 1935 to participate in the confrontation between a rebellious segment of the population and government troops in Mahshad; one of Reza Shah's attempts at modernising the country which ended badly. Among the troops which were despatched from Tehran, was Zulu; the ensuing standoff ended violently, with a large number of dead and injured. It was an event that remained deeply rooted in the national memory and was to embitter relations between the clergy and the Crown thereafter.

***

Aliyar loved hunting, and this had gradually evolved into a sideline that allowed him to pursue a favourite pastime, with no financial strain on us. It also took him back to many parts of the country where he was well-known from his time in the army under Reza Shah. Abundant game and good fishing were to be had if one knew where to go. Word had gotten around among the expatriates that Aliyar knew how to organise a successful shoot and was good company, so he was much in demand. He was very choosy about his clients, and many of them had become friends, as was the case with Dick Duparc, who headed the Iranian office of a large European company.

On one occasion, they were outside a village crouched behind a rock waiting for a leopard, which was doing damage to the villagers' livestock. The leopard crept up from behind them, and Aliyar, more attuned to stealthy movements than Dick, had just enough time to roll over onto his back and fire off a shot as the leopard leapt in an attempt to go over and beyond them; he managed to get in a shot to its throat, and the animal landed dead on top of him. He would not normally have taken a shot that should have been his client's, but it would have been too dangerous to wait for Dick to react.

In a triumphant return from their trip, they came to fetch me from the royal opera house where I was attending a performance. The dead leopard had been propped up on its hindquarters on the roof of the jeep, and it looked for all the world as if Aliyar was riding around with a dangerous and unleashed live animal on the top of his jeep. We had the skin treated, and it lay splayed out on the floor of our living room.

Dick offered Aliyar a position with the company, which pleased us both, as they got along well. We hoped it would put us on a more stable financial footing than the seesaw of the day-to-day fortunes of the restaurant, and we thought we could look forward to a normal social life, which the hours we'd kept at Le Bistrot had not allowed. It was quite usual for a foreign company to have a capable, well-connected local for liaison work, and it was the sort of work with which Aliyar was familiar and at which he excelled.

During this time, we went to Ziba-Kenar, a resort on the Caspian, where Dick had friends. While staying there, I made the acquaintance of a fisherman who was persuaded to let me be present when he brought in a sturgeon. In the early hours of the morning, I stood in a hut and watched the entire process of extracting and treating the precious roe. He allowed me to be present while he slit open the carcass and continued with his preparations. But there was one last secret he would not share. Like the sorcerer's apprentice, I never learnt the most important part of the formula, the one that would have made me into a genuine magician.

It surprises me now that Aliyar, normally so quick in his perceptions, took some months to arrive at the conclusion that however effective he himself was in his professional capacity, there had been a hidden personal agenda when Dick had offered Aliyar the job. He liked Dick, and I think he did not want to admit to himself or to me, to his disappointment in the man. Dick's own position as head of a company with important contracts in Iran would have ensured that he was introduced to the right people and invited everywhere. Aliyar's friendship with, and access to, these same people was based neither on wealth nor position but rather on an elaborate web of tribal connections and shared histories, which were nurtured rather than discarded by each succeeding generation – this was no longer as evident in Western society but remained one of the cornerstones of Iranian society and culture. As Aliyar's dependents, Taïssia and I were also accorded the protection enjoyed by the members of these interlinked circles; my Farsi was fluent after so many years in Iran, and I had formed many independent friendships within those circles. And much as Aliyar might have wanted to deny it, our friendship with Fathollah Amir-Alahi was a powerful attraction for both the Duparcs.

Dick and his wife Poppet were dedicated partygoers and liked to be seen; for the well-heeled and the well-established, Tehran provided many opportunities for both. Dick was a wealthy man in his own right, a bon vivant, and a doting husband who showered Poppet with luxuries. I was already slightly acquainted with Poppet, who used to come to Ninon's beauty salon. She was a slender woman and had no need of the slimming treatments it offered, but it was patronised by quite a few socialites, and one might very well meet and begin there a friendship with women from the 'inner circle'.

After Aliyar started working with Dick, Poppet began inviting me to accompany her on shopping expeditions or for the evening if our husbands were away on hunting or business trips and came to trust me enough to make me her confidante. I liked her well enough and enjoyed having the leisure for frivolous feminine activities. If I found her rather shallow and occasionally patronising, I was also a good deal younger, she was the wife of my husband's boss, and it might not have been that different as Elrikh's or André's wife : there would still have been the senior officers' wives to whom I would have had to defer. Hierarchies exist everywhere.

I had not thought all this merited discussion with Aliyar, until he himself began to voice his growing discomfort with the situation. He did not go into specifics, but if, as was probable, Dick thought that being Aliyar's boss gave him licence to patronise him as Poppet had done with me, a confrontation was inevitable and a dignified resignation preferable. Aliyar left after eighteen months with the company, and though we continued to be friendly with the couple, it was with some reservations. Events in the distant future were to prove these well-founded – the Duparcs, we would learn, were fair-weather friends.

***

We moved from Tehran to Abadan, where our friend Serge Bezrouké owned the only Western-style hotel. He entrusted us with the task of improving and livening up its restaurant as we had done at the Hotel Caspien. Abadan lay at the mouth of the Arvand River, off the old port city of Khorramshahr. The only reasons for the existence of the Abadan International Hotel and everything else in this characterless island city, were the oil refinery and the pipeline that fed it. Both had been built some fifty years earlier, after the discovery in 1908 of Iran's first oilfield, the Masjid-e-Soleiman, slightly to the north of Ahvaz and not very far from Abadan.

The entire area, Khuzestan Province, had been part of the Ottoman Empire until 1847, and its population was predominantly Arabic-speaking. Its chief, Sheikh Khazal, had leased land for that first refinery to the British and, in the process, had negotiated for himself extremely profitable agreements with them. He had done this without reference to the central government, which claimed he owed the national treasury an enormous sum in back taxes. Reza Shah had taken a very dim view of the situation, and Sheikh Khazal, along with the Bakhtiari khans in the neighbouring province of Lorestan, had been among his chief targets when he began curtailing the independence of the tribal leaders after he came to power.

We spent a year in Abadan, and, save for a visit to Kharg island, neither the place, nor our time there offered anything memorable. Taïssia and I went to Kharg at the invitation of the Garagozlou family. Kharg is a long, narrow island in the northern part of the Persian Gulf. Once known for its pearl fisheries, and in spite of being a barren rock where everything had to be brought in by boat, it had been a useful landfall for trading ships. After the discovery of the oilfields and the building of the refinery, extensive facilities had been built there to load oil tankers, with a small landing strip that permitted aircraft to ferry in personnel and supplies.

We were taken there by private helicopter and shown what little there was to see – ruins dating from pre-Islamic times and some pre-Christian graves, though we were not told much else about them. We watched the local women walk out into the shallows and lower inverted pots tied to ropes, bringing them up filled with sweet water from freshwater springs bubbling out into the seabed. Most singular of all were the 'freezing trees'; it was fatal, we were told, to rest in their shade, where it became so cold that one could freeze to death. Though I did not doubt the truth of what they told us, I found it quite hard to imagine such a thing happening in that burning heat. It was a desolate place, made even more unappealing by the machinery and utilitarian buildings. But it was a necessary ugliness because everything in Iran came back to, and depended upon oil, and its crucial role in the economy of the country.

We had done what we could to improve the restaurant, but nothing could change the fact that Abadan itself did not offer the same varied and sophisticated attractions as Tehran, so we were all excited when the time came for us to pack our bags and return there.

Chapter 16

IRANBARITE

It was, once again, Fathollah, tireless in his efforts on our behalf, who had found what he insisted was the perfect opening for Aliyar. He introduced Aliyar to Ali Asghar Pairavi, a likeable young athlete whose family owned a barite mine. As the mineral is used in the oil refining process and is, consequently, a commodity greatly in demand both in Iran and internationally, the Pairavis were set to do very well out of this state of affairs.

They were an old-fashioned family from Shiraz, a city famed for its gardens and its poets; Asghar's courteous manners reflected his old-fashioned upbringing, and he spoke no English, had not travelled, and had no knowledge of the world beyond Iran. He was looking for somebody to fill the position of director of sales and public relations in his newly established company, somebody with administrative skills, worldly and sophisticated, whose English was fluent enough to meet clients and conduct negotiations. During the course of their first meeting he said to Aliyar, 'You'll make the company grow, and I will grow with it.'

The new company, Iranbarite, started out modestly from a small suite of offices that was actually a residential apartment, with five staff – Asghar and Zulu, myself as secretary, an accountant, and a chauffeur cum general factotum. Apart from the national refineries, Iranbarite's biggest client was in the United States, and Zulu often had to attend business meetings in Texas as well as in Europe.

It was the usual practice for wealthy Iranians to send their children abroad for a university education, if not for their schooling. For the less well-off, there was recourse to the scholarships awarded by the state, but even with this assistance, sending a child to study abroad could place great financial strain on a family, as the salaries and earnings of middle-class families in Iran were considerably lower than were those of similarly placed families in the West. The Pairavis had no such constraints, but, rather curiously, they had chosen to send not their son but their daughter, Parvané, abroad for her education. It struck me as unusual because it was a society in which sons were favoured and given priority over daughters. So it was surprising that the Pairavis, who were so traditional that they seemed a little out of place even in Tehran, should choose to act in a way that appeared to give their daughter an advantage over their son. Moreover, their sending her abroad meant she would not be as strictly supervised as she would have been in their household. The only explanation that seemed to make sense to me at the time was that they wanted their daughter to acquire the sophistication and accomplishments that had become de rigueur for young women of good families in their rapidly changing world but wanted their son to remain at home, the better to establish himself and to familiarise himself with both the business and the people who would help him to achieve success.

Parvané was a little younger than her brother, in her late teens or early twenties when I first met her. She was on a short visit from England, where she was studying, and had brought along her pet poodle, who scampered about the Pairavi household annoying the servants and most particularly the old maidservant who had come with them from Shiraz. She detested the dog, muttering and complaining about the 'little nuisance' and the extra work she had to do because of him.

The visit provided us with amusement for many weeks after Asghar reported that the dog had found its way into a small room set aside for prayers, where some holy stones brought back from a pilgrimage to Mecca were kept in a shrine; he grabbed one in his mouth and raced off to play with it in the courtyard. The old maidservant came in to dust the room, noted a stone was missing, and saw the dog in the courtyard pushing the stone about with his nose, as she was on her way to report the stone's disappearance to her mistress. When she tried to take the precious pebble away from him, the dog thought she was trying to play with him and kept on jumping up and running around her in circles, holding the stone in his mouth all the while. She set up a hue and cry, and when the family went to investigate the reason for the uproar, found her screeching imprecations and curses at him, calling him *Sheitan Najess* (filthy devil) as she hobbled after him trying to retrieve the holy stone. We always referred to the poodle by that nickname from then on.

Mrs. Pairavi, with all her traditional values, was not averse to cheating at cards and was nicknamed 'the toad' by the ladies of her circle.

***

Iranbarite was doing extremely well and had a growing reputation for supplying high quality raw material; in fact it had expanded so much that Asghar decided to buy an entire building to house the new offices and staff. Asghar also decided that we should be lodged in keeping with the status he believed his company now enjoyed; he moved us to a luxurious house with a large garden and an immense pool where we could entertain in the lavish manner that was the norm in the oil industry and, therefore, expected of the chief representative of Iranbarite. This unnecessarily large and overstated house in fashionable Niyavaran might not have been our choice, but Asghar felt it was necessary to maintain the company's high-profile image, and neither of us was complaining.

The pool was Zulu's cherished domain. In hot weather, when time permitted, he was most often to be found with whichever of our friends was prepared to take him on at chess, both of them comfortably settled on inflatable stools at the shallow end of the pool, each with a drink at his elbow, contemplating contentedly and with intense concentration a chessboard set up on a floating platform between them. Zulu had suffered the sudden and violent loss of many relatives and of other people close to him too; there had been upheavals and privations and then the final disappointment of having to leave the Legion, with part of a lung cut out and a couple of fingers missing. He had put hard work and dedication into making a success of Iranbarite, and I felt happy and secure as I watched him, believing that, at last, our lives rested on a stable foundation. I should have known better.

Our life took on a more settled rhythm. I was no longer working at Iranbarite. We had Marie, a Russian-speaking maid, to help in the house. And we acquired our own dogs, including a dachshund called Atussa. Taïssia was now old enough not to need my constant presence; she was busy with her own circle of friends, many of them classmates from the Lycée Français.

Friday is the day of rest in Muslim countries, so the weekend fell on a Thursday and Friday rather than on a Saturday and Sunday as in Christian countries. Taïssia was of the same age as Princess Ashraf's daughter, Dottie, and the two girls usually spent Thursdays together at the princess's palatial residence. Naturally, this friendship would not have been allowed to develop had the princess not approved of us or of Taïssia as a suitable companion for her daughter.

To my delight, I discovered that Nicole Douzedamme, my old classmate from the Collège Fénélon in Cambrai, lived in Tehran. She was now the wife of an Iranian businessman, who just happened to be Iranbarite's competitor. Unperturbed by our husbands' rivalries, she invited me to dinner when Zulu was away on a business trip. Social circles in Tehran were small enough for Asghar to hear of it. He was outraged and horrified until I explained the circumstances and assured him that it was a matter of a friendship from my teens and had nothing to do with business.

I now had plenty of free time, and Zulu would occasionally take me with him when he travelled to France on business. We went often enough to become quite well-known at the Paris Hilton, where we were always treated very well. On one of these trips I made the acquaintance of Alain Ousmane, a Franco-Sudanese arms dealer, when Zulu and I stopped by at his flat come office on the Champs-Elysées. Ousmane turned out to be a sympathetic man who had known the Zulgadars when they lived on Avenue Henri Martin. We got along quite well, and after that, he would invite me for a meal or a drink whenever I was in Paris, usually arranging to meet at Fouquets, which was just below his flat.

When I got to know him better, I once asked him why he had no family, and his answer was that he was afraid of the possibility that his own mixed parentage might result in his paternal genes emerging strongly in any child of his. He was convinced that this would affect the child's future. How unfortunate, I thought, that he should feel that way and deny himself the pleasures of a family, as he seemed to have done well enough in business in spite of his mixed blood. Alain Ousmane became persona non grata in Iran after he was named in an arms scandal, and I eventually lost touch with him.

***

Zulu and I both suffered the loss of a parent during these years. My father-in-law suffered a massive heart attack while driving his jeep on a trip north. The car was found with his body and that of the chauffeur, also dead, next to him. It is probable that he took the wheel before the heart attack which caused the vehicle to go out of control and crash.

My mother died in Paris, but I was not to know this until many weeks later. My father later told me that, when he found out that Zulu was away in Texas, he decided not to inform me of her illness because he knew that I would not be able to leave Iran without my husband's permission. He felt that there was no need for me to suffer the anguish of not being able to come to Paris while she was failing, so he waited until Zulu had returned to inform us.

I flew to Paris some months later, and Papa and I made a visit to the Russian cemetery in Sainte Geneviève-des-Bois. We wandered around looking for Maman's grave, but he could not find the way to it. Our family plot was located next to the grave of General Zouboff, my father's companion at the taxi rank in Montmartre, the same family friend who had often given me a lift home so many years earlier. We went back to find the caretaker, and embarrassed to admit that he could no longer remember the way to his late wife's grave, Papa asked him 'Please could you tell me where General Zouboff is?'

'He's not gone anywhere as far as I know,' said the man dryly.

Inappropriate though it might have been in such a solemn place, Papa and I both burst out laughing before explaining what we wanted, and we made our way to Maman's grave after the caretaker told us where to go.

I suspected that Papa had not waited long before looking for consolation after, if not before, my mother's death, and this was confirmed when I discovered that his mistress had moved into the flat with him shortly after my mother's death. She had kept what she wanted and had thrown out the rest of my mother's things without waiting to consult my father or me. It was too late to make an issue of it, and I returned to Tehran disappointed not to have any mementoes of my mother.

Though I am not sure whether the woman actually entered Papa's life before or after Maman's death, I had known from a young age that he was not entirely faithful to Maman, however much he cherished her. I could also see that age was beginning to take its toll, and I realised how vulnerable he had now become. This realisation did not prevent me from feeling angry with him for showing such weakness in allowing her to behave unilaterally and for not having taken a stand in this regard.

***

When Zulu was not travelling, we often used to go north to the shores of the Caspian; we usually stayed at the hotel in Ramsar, once a private residence built by Reza Shah. The landscape around the estate with its imposing buildings was quite beautiful, with streams bubbling through the woods and sloping down to the littoral and wildfowl in abundance everywhere. Zulu would go hunting, and I would usually stroll about the grounds, where I once came across a pen with a bear prowling by its railings. His keeper told me that he had a fondness for tobacco and was waiting for passers-by to give him a cigarette. I handed one out of my handbag to the keeper, who gave it to the bear. The animal proceeded to chew it with apparent relish. Thereafter, I used to bring the bear a cigarette every time we visited Ramsar. Naturally, the keeper was given a few for himself as well.

***

Zulu had kept in touch with one of his clients from his hunting days, Kurt Tschudi, who was also a keen aviator and came to Iran piloting his own airplane. Kurt and his wife invited us to stay with them in Switzerland. He had just acquired a new aircraft shortly before we arrived and was trying it out as Mrs Tschudi and I watched him coming in for a landing.

'I bet he's going to forget that the landing gear on this one's different,' she said, and indeed he did. He neglected to operate the mechanism to lower the wheels, and they did not come down; the aircraft slid across the runway on its belly. I dread to think of the cost of repairing it, if that was at all possible, and was relieved that he was a sufficiently good flier to have avoided further and more serious mishap.

The Tschudis had a Doberman who would accompany them when they went out into the town centre. After a while, he would take off on his own, climb onto the tram, get off at the correct stop, and trot home. It cost nothing, and the tram drivers were quite used to him. One day, he got off at the wrong stop, the last one on a route that ended outside the zoo. The poor animal did not know where he was and wandered around until somebody noticed and reported him; the Tschudis had been waiting at home for him to return, worried and anxious, until they received a call from the police.

***

There was some excitement over a commodity from the humid hinterland along the Caspian – freshwater shrimp. They were found living in ponds fed by the springs. We were told there was great demand in Scandinavia for them. The news inspired Zulu to attempt to enter the field himself – with his contacts, he was sure we could become big exporters ourselves. It could not be difficult, he thought, but how were we to obtain the shrimp? And where were we to raise them? The freshwater ponds in which they could be raised required land, which he did not have, and even if he did, it was too risky to throw over a perfectly good job to move to the shores of the Caspian.

He came up with a novel idea that did not require a great deal of money or our departure from Tehran. We would make an experimental attempt to raise them at home, and if that worked, we could consider how to take the idea further. Guests visiting our spare bathroom were startled to find the bathtub full of live shrimp. Alas, the experiment was not successful and we abandoned it after some months. But it was fun while it lasted!

***

Our friend Karin Stephen had been widowed when Henry, still a young man, died of a heart attack; Karin was left to bring up their three daughters on her own. The State Department of the United States offered her a job in its cultural arm, the United States Information Service. She was posted to Tehran, and we were thrilled to see her and her three daughters again. She and I would often take trips to our favourite haunts on the Caspian, sometimes with the girls in the back of her station wagon, usually to Ramsar or Zeba Kenar.

The arrival of Ninon's brother, Dodo, and his English wife, Beryl, occasioned comment and quite a lot of mirth. Dodo had played minor roles in films, including *Doctor Zhivago*. Dodo and Beryl drove to Iran in a sand-coloured Rolls-Royce they'd bought as an investment in England. The vehicle had, apparently, been ordered by an Arab prince who did not eventually take delivery of it. That accounted for its colour, appropriate to the sands of the desert it never saw. There were potential buyers enough in a country where ostentation was the norm and people with new money were not shy about flaunting it. After Beryl and Dodo sold it, they were often to be seen on a scooter on their way to a reception, Dodo in a dinner jacket with Beryl riding pillion, her evening gown gathered up around her knees.

Business at Iranbarite was flourishing, but I thought Zulu ought to be wary of the accountant and said as much to him. I believed the man to be ambitious and unscrupulous, and this assessment proved correct when he manoeuvred Zulu out of a job, making Zulu's position so untenable that he was obliged to leave the company. It was a bitter end to ten years of building up a business and its reputation from scratch. I felt Zulu had been rash in his handling of a showdown with Asghar and the accountant, but saying 'I told you so' did not give me much satisfaction or change the situation. He was blithe in his conviction that something else would come along without delay.

It was all very well to be so sanguine about the future, but I was getting a little tired of Zulu's lack of caution and his reckless disregard of all consequences. In spite of my misgivings, our luck held.

Chapter 17

DIZINE

His Majesty's early years at his Swiss boarding school had resulted, among other things, in his becoming a keen and proficient skier. Iran had a suitable climate and slopes but no facilities for the sport. A resort was created at Dizine, a couple of hours' drive north of Tehran, where skiers could enjoy an exceptionally long season. Ninon's husband, Felix Aghayan, put us in charge of the luxurious hotel he'd built there. Its accommodation included a royal suite, which was destined for the use of Their Majesties and their children. To Felix's disappointment, however, the family always used their own chalet a thousand metres farther up.

I would go up to the chalet to oversee the arrangements when they visited and was sometimes there at mealtimes, when I observed that the family usually conversed in French when among themselves. It could have been to give the children practice in a language both Their Majesties spoke fluently. On the other hand, it could have been in order to communicate more freely in front of the staff, though many members of their entourage, including, of course, the children's French governess, would have had no difficulty in following their conversation. How like old Russia, I thought, though it must be said that, unlike a lot of Russian aristocrats, the family spoke Farsi as well, whereas the Russians had often not spoken Russian, though it was supposedly their own language, and many of them mangled the language if they did speak it at all.

Dizine was close enough to Tehran for me to make short trips there. On the odd occasion, I would return earlier than expected. Then the housekeeping staff would scurry about as soon as they saw my car drawing up and would usually be waiting for me with urgent questions, apparently insoluble problems, and trivial matters that could easily have been dealt with by Zulu – where was he anyway? It was after a particularly harrowing visit to the capital that I realised that these were merely delaying tactics and discovered the purpose they served.

Head held high was, yet again, the only recourse I had. I had a growing certainty that Zulu strayed, but on one occasion my anger at his behaviour towards Ninon and Felix overrode all else. Not that I expected him to be decorous, which was completely out of character, but this was unforgivable self-indulgence on his part. I had gone to Tehran to be with Ninon after she rang to tell us that her daughter had died of an overdose. My own daughter was proving to be something of a handful, and there were surely occasions when Ninon's had caused her irritation and despair, but that could not lessen a mother's anguish at losing a child. I left for Tehran as soon as I received the news. I had arrived alone at the Aghayan residence and found a solemn and hushed gathering in the family's large salon. Ninon came towards me, held out her arms and hugged me, asking in a broken voice, 'Where's Zulu? Why isn't he with you?'

He had remained in Dizine, saying that we could not both leave the hotel. It was a selfish and cowardly reaction at a time when he should have understood, as I could well see, that, while nothing could bring comfort or consolation, his presence would have made a difference to Ninon, if not to Felix. Expressing my anger towards Zulu would have not have changed anything, not for Ninon and Felix and not for me.

During a particularly cold spell one winter, I was awoken early to be informed that the pipes in the royal chalet had frozen solid overnight. There was a note of panic in the voice of the member of staff who brought me the news, as the royal couple was expected later that day. Accompanied by maids and a couple of strong fellows, I went up to the chalet and instructed them to start pouring hot water down the toilets. Some hours and many bucketsful later, the pipes had thawed out. And we breathed a sigh of relief just as we heard the sound of a helicopter overhead.

Her Majesty arrived first and left for the slopes without dawdling. His Majesty arrived some time later and stopped by the staircase to consult with General Nader Jehanbani, who was accompanying him. I saw him looking towards me and asking a question in a low voice. After HM left to join his wife, we both sat down and decided we deserved a drink, I because I had had a tense and demanding morning and Nader because being in attendance on Their Majesties could have been without its own difficulties. He sent one of the household attendants to look in Her Majesty's case upstairs for a bottle of liqueur – it was either Cointreau or Drambuie, I cannot now remember which. I am embarrassed to admit that we helped ourselves liberally while he chuckled and recounted the exchange between himself and the shah.

'Isn't that Zolqadr's wife?'
Nader had agreed that it was indeed so.
'Still the same one after twenty years?

His Majesty had, quite clearly, known my husband for much longer than I had. He would certainly have known Zulu's first wife quite well and perhaps the second one too.

The first Begum Zulgadar was Tatyana Teimourtash, the widow of a minister of Reza Shah's who had fallen out of favour. It was the fate which befell many, yet another who had drunk the Shah's coffee. While he was still in power and in favour, the man's son had attended Le Rosey with His Majesty, then the crown prince. Zulu was younger than Tatyana, an Armenian and a society beauty. They parted in anger after he behaved rather badly by not turning up at a party she had arranged in honour of his birthday. It was the beginning of autumn, and Zulu himself would rather have gone hunting. Undeterred by her arrangements, he had agreed with his orderly upon a time to wait for him with transport at the corner of the street where they lived. In the early afternoon, Zulu announced that he was popping out to buy a packet of cigarettes from the shop around the corner. He might well have bought the cigarettes for all I know, but instead of going back to the house, he jumped into the waiting jeep and went off on his hunting expedition. I expect he returned as casually as he had left, but the furious and humiliated Tatyana did not forgive him for leaving her to face their guests alone. That was the end of that marriage.

The second Begum Zulgadar had threatened to kill Zulu, so incensed was she with his infidelities; I imagine it mattered not a bit to him, and he continued to behave as he had always done. She was German, and as an enemy alien, she was obliged to leave Iran when the Allies took control of the country during the Second World War. In order to ensure that she made it safely to the border, Zulu travelled with the convoy transporting the group of departing Germans north. They would be repatriated by the Russians, who would meet them and take charge at the border.

Perhaps Zulu was not reassured by the behaviour of the Russian soldiers, or perhaps he thought it was a means of leaving Iran, which he was keen to do. Whatever his reasons, instead of turning back at the border, he crossed with the group of Germans, aroused the suspicions of the Russians, and was thrown into a prison camp. It required the offices of his uncle Assadollah Khan at the Ministry of External Affairs to secure his release and return to Iran.

Shortly after this repatriation, Zulu made another attempt, this time successfully, from another direction and by an entirely different route. A boatman in the south was persuaded to row him across the Tigris to the far side, which brought him into Iraq. He was picked up by the occupying Allied forces, but without suitable identity papers, he once again aroused suspicion. He was sufficiently convincing for them to contact the nearest regiment of the Foreign Legion while he waited in a prison camp until his bona fides could be confirmed. The 13th Half-Brigade of the Foreign Legion was fighting with the Free French in the Middle East, and by a stroke of luck, there were officers in it who had known him and could vouch for him; it turned out to be a shorter-than-expected wait. Armed with a newly issued identity card, Zulu was at last free to join his old comrades. He had already been declared a deserter in Iran, but he was still thrilled to be back where he felt and believed he truly belonged- with his comrades in the Foreign Legion.

The end of the war found him in Germany. His wife might reasonably be expected to have returned to the country. Perhaps she did not make it back, perhaps he could not find her, or perhaps the war took its toll on that relationship as it did of so many others. He never brought up the subject though, so there is no record of what happened to her after their parting in the refugee camp.

He was doing useful work liaising with the Allied Forces, and later assisting them as the reconstruction of the country went forward, but he found peacetime dull and lacklustre. A man of his temperament needed the excitement of action.

When France began marshalling her forces for the Indochinese insurgency, he did not hesitate to resign from his job and make straight for Paris to re-enlist in the Foreign

The Fourth Wife of Aliyar Bey

Legion. He was accepted in spite of his age, and once again, there was a happy reunion with old comrades.

In the short while before the troops left, one of his mates asked for help with a delicate and confidential matter. A childhood friend, a young woman from a prominent family had become pregnant, but the father of the child was not in a position to marry her immediately. The parents were strait-laced and there would be a scandal if they discovered the daughter's condition, so she needed to marry somebody, anybody acceptable to them, before they did. Once the child was born, a divorce would follow, of course. Would Zulu, conveniently single and socially acceptable, gallantly oblige?

Appealed to in this manner, Zulu was agreeable. If he was killed, she would have a widow's pension and the child his name, if perchance its father did not come up to scratch. And if he survived, no harm was done; they would be free of each other by the time he returned.

The wedding took place the day before he left France. As the bride was pregnant and already spoken for by somebody else, Zulu diverted his attentions to the bridesmaid and spent the night before the wedding with her. The matter was neatly resolved, a scandal averted, and a family's honour remained intact, with nobody the wiser. He himself had had some entertainment out of it; had emerged blameless; and did not, it seemed, have a care in the world. He eagerly left the next day to fight in Indochina. This was the third Beghum Zulgadar.

***

I am not intolerant, and what other men did concerned their wives, not me. Neither am I a prig. But Zulu's sense of irresponsibility had begun to wear on me, and this time, I was the wife. I was beginning to discern a pattern of behaviour that worried and dismayed me. On earlier occasions, when I had spoken to Fathi about it, he had always counselled patience and said, 'Don't leave him. Without you, he is a finished man.'

His advice was the same this time. It was not much later, however, that Zulu, completely in keeping with his temperament, became restless and created some upheaval, which ended in our leaving Dizine. Ninon and Felix did not protest, so I suspect that he had done something further to upset them. I felt bad that it should come to this after the unstinting support they had given us. It was once again a return to Tehran, this time to an uncertain future.

A further anxiety in my life was caused by Taïssia, who had become increasingly rebellious. She mixed with the children of some of the richest and most powerful people in the country. When one of her friends was celebrating her eighteenth birthday, there was a grand party, at which the girl's friends admired her parents' present to her – a mink jacket. Taïssia came home thrilled and announced that she too wanted one when she turned eighteen. We had material comforts but were far from having the financial means of the parents of her friend, or indeed of most of the people we knew, and she resented our not being able to give her the same material advantages they had. It was difficult for her to accept that privilege and access to the rich did not automatically mean a fat bank balance.

The jeunesse dorée of the country, children of her generation with very wealthy parents, was one of charming and well-mannered young people, generally a pleasure to meet but indulged beyond what I considered healthy. Apparently limitless allowances from their parents permitted many of them to fritter away their lives fecklessly, many becoming wastrels and spendthrifts, sometimes forming an addiction to drugs and leading fairly uncontrolled lives. They lived in the midst of excess, and it was easy to believe that this charmed generation would never be called to account for anything; nobody appeared to have to do very much to obtain the luxuries, which they took for granted. They were too young to recognise the dangers. And I cannot blame them, for their parents displayed no wisdom either and, more often than not, set a poor example to their children. It was easy to bask in what we believed was a risen sun, nay a still rising sun, little imagining how quickly and dramatically it would set. As Taïssia believed that a life independent of ours would give her greater opportunities than we could, we found her a flat and gave her a substantial sum of money to get her started. It was a greater inheritance than either of us had had, and we wished her joy of it.

Chapter 18

Le Bavaria

Our return to Tehran was followed by a flurry of activity, and I had no time to brood and nurse my sense of malaise. Fathollah had found a basement restaurant that had gone out of business and lay empty. He arranged for us to take it over after we had formed a partnership of three – Zulu and myself, with Fathi as silent partner. I now wonder whether he shared my anxiety and thought that his presence, albeit in the background, would keep a check on Zulu's wilder flights of fancy. Or perhaps he knew something I didn't? Whichever it was, I was relieved to have him on board.

The establishment would need extensive refurbishing, but we were already old hands at that. We kept its name, Le Bavaria, even though that did not reflect the style of restaurant we planned. It was well located to take advantage of the uppermost end of the market; we aimed for guests from the top echelon of government officials and the cream of the business community. In Iran, the two were inextricably linked. The entrance at ground level led downstairs to a bar, beyond which lay the restaurant. A décor of peach, white, and gold was chosen to counteract the effects of the lack of natural light and we hoped the final effect would create a welcoming ambience which would appeal to our guests.

The boom of the last decade showed no signs of slowing down. The majority of the international press was enthusiastic in its praise of the shah and the changing face of the country, which was moving in the direction his father had lain down; the economy was healthy, and money was still pouring in. It was believed that the country was at long last moving towards its destiny, which was to take its rightful place in the forefront of the world's hierarchy. It remained El Dorado, the money needed an outlet, and there was enough optimism for other restaurants to be launched. Their reported success inspired Zo to try her own luck in Tehran. She left France and her smart flat in Paris to live once more under her father's roof. Once there, she had no difficulty finding a restaurant to manage. Her own experience of running an establishment in one of the smartest and busiest areas of Paris, combined with the Zulgadar connections, was reference enough. She took over a restaurant, which she named Xanadu, and turned it into a flourishing business. It became a favourite watering hole for foreign journalists and a meeting place for lunching ladies alike. Under the guidance of the Zulgadar siblings, Xanadu and Le Bavaria, quite different in style, patronage, and décor, both became the most talked about restaurants in the city and the places to be seen. It was a far cry from the days of our nervous beginnings at Le Bistrot in the Hotel Caspien. We had what promised to be another success and could be proud of that, at least.

On a more personal level, I cannot say that we were blissfully happy. But neither of us was behaving with hostility towards the other. There was still a residual attachment between us, there was too much to do, and we simply did not have the time to quarrel. We had, however, adjusted our way of working and, consequently, our timetable. One of us would be in attendance during the day and the other in the evening. Though it was not a hard and fast rule and we were often there together, particularly in the evenings, it meant that I would more often than not take the day shift and Zulu the evening. It happened gradually that we decided we could not both be away from the restaurant together and so we began taking our annual holiday separately. I generally went to Paris and often to the Côte d'Azur, where I knew a lot of people. Zulu would usually go to Vietnam; I am sure it was greatly changed from the days when he was there and it was still called Indochina, but those old haunts were imbued with nostalgia for him and he kept on going back, looking for I knew not what. Did he really believe he could relive the glory days by returning to the scene? His comrades had left with the other French troops – many were in Europe – so he could as easily have exchanged reminiscences with them without returning to the scene of his final and most serious injuries. I did not understand why he did, it but neither did I question it. That would have been a waste of time.

With a portion of a lung missing, Zulu had long ago been advised by his doctors in France and in Iran to give up smoking and to keep his drinking within reasonable limits. He did neither. In fact, he chain-smoked, and his drinking had increased. He was a man of mature years who was not in the best of health but retained the enthusiasm of an adolescent; restraint and control were definitely not his strong suit. To expect either of him would bring nothing but disappointment. Whether it was the drinking or a sign of the advancing years, I noted that his stories had assumed new flourishes and an extravagance that had grown in the telling. More often than not, I knew the original anecdote was far less exciting and colourful than he made it sound. He was still a genial host, remained popular, and was greatly in demand as a raconteur. That only encouraged him in his other excesses.

Occasionally our guests would do something that surprised us, and one of these was ex-King Constantine of Greece. He was visiting Their Majesties, both of whom he counted good friends. I am not sure how it came about that he ended up in the kitchen, but that is where I found him when I arrived at the restaurant one evening. He and Zulu were absorbed in their separate tasks. He may once have been called Your Majesty, but at that moment he was busy frying potatoes while Zulu was supervising the preparation of the grilled meats. Lest anybody have any doubts on the subject, the cooks were well able to perform that very job, and we were not in the habit of making our guests slave for their supper! It has been my destiny to know men who both enjoyed and were good at cooking – my father, Zulu, and now here was a former king who, whether from whim or bonhomie, had invaded my kitchen without ceremony. Whichever it was, we appreciated his informal manner and apparent enjoyment in this most mundane of tasks.

Among the most regular of our patrons was Dr Khodadad Farman-farmaian, governor of the Central Bank of Iran. He came from an eminent family that had long been influential in the political life of the country. His father had been prime minister briefly early in the twentieth century. He would saunter over from his office for lunch every day, never varying his choice. Not everybody who came to have a drink in the bar of Le Bavaria was there to patronise the restaurant. There were some who became fixtures, looking in for a glass or two on most evenings, and it often felt more like a club than a bar open to the public. As with all drinking establishments where people feel comfortable, they would often be there until well after what should have been closing time. Many of them came because they wanted to have a private chat with one of us or because they wanted Zulu's advice on some matter. Tehran may have been a city of several million people, but it was socially quite small and almost everybody knew everybody else; our patrons were often people with whom we mixed away from the restaurant. Many of them had made confidants of us.

I walked in one evening to find one of these regulars sitting glumly at the bar. Two or three others sat around him, all of them looking sympathetic. As I came closer I saw the top two buttons of his shirt undone as he showed them a thick chain around his neck. When I saw that and from its muted gleam, I knew immediately what had happened; he had been awarded what Zulu and I jocularly and very privately referred to as 'The Order of the Platinum Chain.'

He had been the companion of a rich socialite. A divorcée from an eminent family, she liked to be escorted by men younger than herself, always well-connected and preferably good-looking. When she decided it was time for a change, she was in the habit of bidding the incumbent farewell by presenting him with a platinum chain. He was not the first I had seen like this. There had been other stricken men with bruised egos, feeling humiliated after having received their marching orders from the same lady. Of course I was suitably consolatory and did not let my cynicism or amusement show. There was no reason why our sympathy should prevent us from seeing the comic aspect of the situation. They all thought they would last longer than their predecessors. How could they be so naive, each and every one? In hindsight, the same could be said of me, for eventually I too was naive and trusting.

***

I received a call from Zo asking me to be at lunch at Xanadu on a particular day. Her Majesty the Shahbanou was to be there with a small party of other women, and Zo wanted to make sure that an appropriate clientele would be occupying the other tables. I knew it was usual for the palace to vet the bookings in advance, and there, I was a known entity. Her Majesty's table had been placed just a little apart, where the other guests could not overhear their conversation, though it was quite unobtrusively organized. All was proceeding normally until a cat somehow found its way in from the courtyard and jumped onto the Shahbanou's table. Amazement all around and a moment of stunned silence followed, until the cat was shooed out of the restaurant, after which there was a burst of relieved laughter. I wonder whether any of the people present that day still remembers that little incident? Her Majesty was certainly gracious about it at the time. It is not one of the best moments for a restaurateur, but as there were no repercussions from the palace or reports in the press, neither the reputation nor the popularity of the restaurant suffered in consequence.

And then the Russian circus came to town. It was a wonderful spectacle and a popular attraction. However, as the performers could not afford to eat at the restaurant, we invited them all to our house instead. It was a rowdy evening, as was to be expected with so many Slavs.

The Italian ambassador and his wife, Luigi and Lili Cottafari, hosted a sumptuous alfresco banquet with the décor done in a style reminiscent of the eighteenth century, the waiting staff all gloved and bewigged and suitably attired. I call the style Louis XV, but I suppose as an Italian, the ambassador meant to recreate an approximation of the luxury of Venice, which he had to do without the canals, of course. It may well have been Lili, who was of aristocratic Austrian stock, who had provided the inspiration for it. It was, at any rate, a memorable evening, and though I cannot now recollect the dishes we had, they were very sumptuous too. But I do remember what a glamorous occasion it was, and I also remember being seated next to Khodadad Farman-farmaian's wife, who was accompanied by one of

The Fourth Wife of Aliyar Bey

their daughters, both Mrs Farman-farmaian and I without our husbands.

Thinking now about that banquet, at which there were no masks, and a trip to Venice, which I enjoyed, I am reminded of a masked costume ball at the palace. Some imaginative costumes were in evidence, but most of us were sufficiently well-acquainted with one another, and I do not think anybody was actually taken in by the 'disguises' or confused by the masks. That did not detract from the fact that the opportunity to indulge in a bit of fantasy is always welcome. Certainly Ninon did not fool an old friend; as His Majesty swept past her while dancing with somebody or other, he murmured with a smile, 'Bonsoir, Miss Dior.' It was the fragrance she always wore, recognisable to all her circle.

Owning a restaurant means there are always surprises, and a happy one was the arrival of a pair of guests I could not have imagined meeting – Frank Sinatra and Spiro Agnew. Sinatra was in Tehran to sing at a huge charity event in aid of Her Majesty's pet cause, and Agnew's visit coincided with that. After their visit to Le Bavaria, they invited me out for a meal. I took a well-earned evening off and spent it being greatly entertained, as both actor-entertainer and politician were consummate performers in their different ways. Of course, we were hounded by photographers, but both men were accustomed to the attention. Whether as a model or as owner-manager of a restaurant, one is always on display, so it was not unfamiliar territory for me, even though I was not the celebrity.

Chapter 19

GATHERING CLOUDS AND A FINAL PARTING

Tehran, 1976–Paris, 1979

Managing a restaurant is time-consuming, but the shenanigans and entertaining doings of our patrons at Le Bavaria were not enough to distract me from what was happening in our private lives. These seemed to be diverging; we were drifting apart with increasing rapidity. This was something more than the familiarity born of over twenty years together. We still shared more than a roof together, but a restlessness in Zulu was unsettling both of us. While he was the more flamboyant of the two of us, I did not lack attention or admirers. That had never been an issue for me; neither had it been difficult to discourage any attempts at intimacy. But the niggling discontent that had become part of my life from the time we lived in Dizine was intensifying.

Preoccupied as I was with the day-to-day matters of managing a business, I still had time to note the alarming level of Zulu's drinking and smoking, the minor incidents that had become major events I no longer recognised in the telling, the behaviour that seemed manic. I, pretty much like everybody else, did not sense the discontent that was growing outside our walls and beyond our own relatively unimportant lives. In the not so far distance, storm clouds were gathering. We were too caught up in our own existences to understand they were headed our way.

The final nail in the coffin was Zulu's behaviour at a party in our house. It became evident that he was involved with one of our guests; I caught them in flagrante. It was an insult that I was not going to put up with in my own house. It did not take long or much persuasion for me to take up the invitation of one of our French patrons, a diplomat who had pursued me unsuccessfully until then.

Zulu and I agreed that a trial separation would give us time to consider how we wanted to deal with our marriage. I accompanied my diplomat, who was on the verge of leaving Tehran to take up a new posting in Pakistan, while Zulu stayed in Tehran to run the restaurant.

It was three years before my lover ended our relationship, with cowardice and a complete lack of grace. This time it was not finding him in the arms of another woman that drove me away; that would have been the easy way out, for him at least. It was left to two friends in Paris to tell me on a visit there that I was no longer wanted back in Pakistan; not having the courage to tell me himself, he had asked them to convey the message on his behalf.

I started looking for a job and was dismayed that none of our friends from Tehran could prove helpful; I was no longer of use to anybody, it seemed. I had kept in touch with the Duparcs; I met Poppet a few times, but she was obvious in her lack of interest, and her husband, Dick, when I approached him for a job, made a few weak excuses and declined to be of any assistance. Zulu and I were not wrong in our assessment of the couple.

It was my modelling experience and knowledge of fashion and clothes that proved to be an asset. I found a job as assistant buyer for the women's department of the Paris store of a large European chain. I had kept my parents' old apartment in Clichy, so with a roof and a job, at least I could keep body and soul together.

Just as I thought I was as settled as I could be, Iran fell prey to fundamentalists and the shah was obliged to leave the country. Fortunately, Taïssia had already left for the United States, and I finally had news from Zulu, who would ring late at night or in the early hours of the morning.

Whenever Zulu rang, he would caution me to stay away from Iranians who might not be as straightforward as they appeared to be – there was no way of knowing whether these people, whom we had met as close acquaintances if not close friends in Tehran, were under pressure from the new regime.

He also advised me not to make any changes to the registration of my parents' flat and telephone, both of which were still listed under Ponomareff.

Shortly after that, he rang to let me know that the restaurant had been looted and burnt by rioting crowds, with special attention given to the stocks of liquor. He himself was ringing from the living room, where he sat facing the door of our flat with a loaded gun. He was a marked man.

I was worried when no further news came. But it would turn out that I'd heard nothing because he had managed to leave Iran – again clandestinely, though that was hardly surprising. He refused to tell me how that had been accomplished, who had helped him, or what route he had taken when he turned up in Paris. He was in France for a few weeks prior to going on to Spain, where many exiled Iranians had found refuge and among whom he had friends. We met on a few occasions while he was in Paris, the first time being at Fouquets after I finished work. I brought along my boss, partly to introduce them and partly for moral support. She realised his embarrassment when it was time to pay the bill and quickly insisted on paying it herself. I was grateful for her sensitivity because he obviously did not have much money. On another occasion, we were on the same train on our way to attend a wedding outside Paris. On the way back, we found ourselves in an empty compartment, and the inevitable happened. But I was still not prepared to trust him or go back to him. At any rate, not being one to remain long without the company of a woman, Zulu already had somebody else in his life, not that it had made a difference to either of us on this particular occasion.

He finally left to go to southern Spain and join his friends. I did not see him again but came to learn that he had been diagnosed with cancer. I left France and went to join Taïssia in New York.

Some months later, a call from the French consulate there informed me of Zulu's death. I was devastated because, whatever our differences, I was not indifferent to him and we had shared many years together. Taïssia was harsh in her judgment of him, and we exchanged strong words. I left her flat and fled to Karin Stephen. I have not seen Taïssia since. Neither do I wish to do so.

I had kept in touch with Zo and discovered that she believed it was likely that her brother had taken his own life; the pain of the disease could well have been too great for him to bear. We agreed to repatriate his body to France, but it was not to be; the Spanish government would not release his body for ten years, or so we understood. He was buried in Spain in the cemetery in Benalmádena.

I too believe that Zulu had taken his life, having decided to take control at the end, after having been tossed about by fate from his early years.

Hélène concludes her account here.

Chapter 20

THE NARRATOR RETURNS TO LA METAIRIE

Mathilde had asked me to spend a few days at La Métairie just before the book was released. My visit would coincide with a reception she had organised to celebrate an award to her son, the architect Yves Lebrun. The book would be published as a collaboration between herself and Hélène, with credit to me as translator. As I was neither the instigator of nor the driving spirit behind the project, I considered this fair. The credit for that went to Mathilde, without whose material contribution and encouragement nothing would have been begun, let alone completed, so it seemed appropriate. She had shown a generosity bordering on the extravagant with my fee. The royalties would be shared between herself, Hélène, and a retirement home for the Foreign Legionnaires. Mathilde's share was the smallest of the three, with the bulk of the royalties going to Hélène. Even with that, this last share to the Foreign Legion would be a handsome sum if the book did well, and I said as much.

'It felt right, and I haven't done this for the money. You knew that from the start. It was Hélène's wish to include the retired legionnaires' home, which she thought would have pleased Zulu. And it's a good idea. As you know, I am already quite comfortably provided for.'

From a caterer's van that stood in the rear courtyard, crates of drinks and crockery were being unloaded and carried to tables already set up on the terrace. I looked at this activity and asked, 'How many people have you invited, Mathilde? I thought you said a small gathering.'

'Around fifty or sixty I think, mostly Yves' team and his old mates. Obviously Hosna and I can't handle such a big affair by ourselves. Besides, I have every intention of enjoying myself at my first party since going to hospital. Tomorrow, you and I are going to see Hélène. We're having lunch at her house; Jean-Paul has an errand to run nearby, so he'll drop us on the way. There's a Georgian couple coming with her, distant cousins who might feel a bit lost, so could you make sure they're all right, please? And I also have an admission to make; now don't get upset. I haven't said anything yet about your visit to Málaga. I thought Hélène ought to hear it at first-hand.'

What a cop out, I thought, though I could not blame her for doing what I had hoped to get away with myself.

***

Roussoudan and Shalva, the Georgian cousins, had brought along Lika, their teenaged daughter. They were both doctors recently arrived in France and working at a hospital southeast of Paris. His mother had been a Nutsubidze, making her Hélène's first cousin; they were meeting Hélène for the first time and staying with her for a few days. I noticed he addressed her as Aunt. The four of us were at sea amid talk of innovative design and the aesthetic merits of various building materials, so we retreated to a quiet corner of the terrace for most of the evening; the other guests were either Yves's old pals or part of the team that had worked on the award-winning building. Shalva kept on wandering off with a video camera. I asked Roussoudan whether she thought there was a resemblance between Shalva and his maternal grandfather, who was also Hélène's uncle. Apart from the information that Hélène's mother, Vera, had been born in Koutaïssi, I did not learn anything of relevance. I had no notion of the geography of the country and resolved privately to consult a map of Georgia.

'Come to Georgia when we return, and we'll show you whatever we can. Things are getting a little tense there at the moment though,' they both said.

Later, when the other guests had left and we sat contentedly sipping Armagnac on the terrace, Shalva asked whether there was a guitar in the house. Yves fetched a handsome specimen, chuckling as he admitted that at school he had been viewed as an eccentric misfit for preferring classical music and an acoustic guitar instead of attempting the latest hits on an electric instrument. Roussoudan tuned it and sang a couple of Georgian songs. She had a fine contralto, and the haunting melodies were the perfect note on which to end the evening.

At noon the next day, some bottles of wine and a large basket were loaded in the boot, a bunch of flowers from the garden placed on top. I had no opportunity to look around when we entered the house, as Hélène led us straight to the kitchen where Jean-Paul deposited the basket, brought in the bottles, and left for his lunch with the tractor dealer, promising to be back in a couple of hours.

Roussoudan and Shalva were out for the day, and it would be just the three of us, which, I am sure, was the way Mathilde had planned it. I watched as an amazing amount of food was swiftly unpacked. There were fresh vegetables, which were tended by Hosna on a patch nestling inside a stone enclosure, once a goose pen, some distance from the house. But that was not all. An astonishing succession of containers and tins, including a pack of tins of cat food followed. This last was placed on a shelf by the window, and all the containers save one were deposited in the fridge or the freezer. That went into the oven, so I assumed it was lunch. The two women chatted animatedly by the sink about the previous evening. One washed salad leaves, while the other made a dressing and sliced vegetables and bread. I sat at the table and observed them without paying heed to their conversation. Hélène laughed – a curious unmusical sound at such odds with her refined appearance that it brought to mind a peacock's raucous call. Surely she won't take it too badly, I was thinking, after all, she was the one who left him. I recalled the barely controlled fury in her voice when she said, 'I wasn't going to stand for that kind of behaviour, not in my own house.' My assumption proved to be a misjudgement, and her anger did not override all other emotions, as I discovered a short while later.

A starter of sliced fresh tomatoes with a dressing of anchovies, parsley, and olive oil was followed by a dish of succulent chicken cooked in a mustardy sauce. One of her favourites, Hélène told me. A green salad and cheese brought lunch to a close, as none of us was partial to sweets. The meal was served with as much ceremony as is possible in a small kitchen. I should have preferred a little more informality but realised that it was, in part, my generation that had dispensed with what was now considered excessive fuss and also that Hélène could not have many opportunities to entertain and was enjoying this occasion to do so, modest though it was.

I was relieved when, lunch over, Mathilde suggested I wait in the salon while they cleared away. I offered to do that as I had not yet made any contribution to the meal and I did not want Mathilde to overtire herself two days in a row. They shooed me out of the kitchen towards the salon across the corridor – a grand name for a tiny gloomy room. It had an out-of-use fireplace that held a gas heater, a small sofa, and two armchairs, one of them of the type called a Voltaire, covered in deep red velvet. On one wall there hung a brightly coloured drawing of the kind prepared by designers to depict a costume. Two watercolours hung on another wall, but it was the framed photos on the mantelpiece and on occasional tables around the room that caught my attention. Some I recognised from the ones Mathilde had put on CD for me; others were new to me. I spotted one of an older Karin Stephen and her daughters, I supposed, and then began looking closely at one of the watercolours. Mathilde and Hélène came in with a tray of coffee cups while I was trying to make out the signature.

'André Montagné,' Hélène said. 'He gave me that one when he had a show in Paris. He had found his rich wife and retired from the legion by then. And that one is by André Vakyevitch.' She indicated the drawing on the wall. 'Eh bien, after what we've done together, both of you now know as much about my life as I do myself. Now, what do you think of the cover design my dear? I quite like it.' She handed me a cup of coffee and reached for a cigarette and her holder after seating herself in the red armchair. Mathilde took the other one and I sat back on the sofa.

'Mmm.' I nodded in agreement but said no more; my opinion was definitely not what mattered here.

Hélène had shown great trust in allowing somebody who was not a close friend to enter an intimately revealing part of her life. The experience had been akin to that of reading a private diary. Mathilde was already familiar with many of the events and anecdotes that had taken place, but for me it had been a time fraught with doubt. Sorting out the wheat from the chaff of the story had required patience and perseverance, and I hoped

I had not missed anything significant and had been sensitive in my handling of her account.

A cat wandered in and made herself comfortable in my lap.

'I hope you don't mind Fifi-jaan? She's very friendly and well-mannered, unlike the other two.'

'They don't like strangers?'

'Sasha and Duschka are shy because they were rescued from a rubbish bin as kittens. What a pitiful state they were in when my neighbour brought them here. They do pretty much as they please all day long and only come in at night.' Then, turning to her friend, 'The Georgian cousins enjoyed your party very much, Mathilde. Thank you once again for including them. I expect they'll phone you when they're back this evening. They've gone to the coast today so I hope the weather holds. They're both greatly appreciated at the hospital,' she added proudly, 'probably because they volunteer for the shifts nobody else will take.'

Estranged as she was from her own child, I could see how pleased she was with the success of these young relatives, however distant the relationship..

I waited for some indication from Mathilde, just as she said, 'Hélène-jaan, there is something you should know.'

Her use of a Farsi term of endearment at this juncture was quite calculated, I thought, particularly as she had admitted to a scant familiarity with the language. Whether this endearment would actually mitigate the effect of what I was going to say was doubtful. I still did not know Hélène well enough to anticipate that. Luis was right; there was no delicate way of telling it. So I launched miserably into my recital, recounting the story of my futile search and ending with the reply he had received from the municipality.

'So, you see, that's why there is no grave any longer,' I ended and watched helplessly as first an incredulous and then a devastated expression crossed her face and tears began to gather in her eyes. Is it possible to suffer the same bereavement a second time? That is how it appeared to me.

Finally, with tears spilling down her cheeks, 'How shameful that nobody told us,' she murmured. Her face still suffused with emotion, she wiped her eyes and composed herself as she continued, 'If only we had known, we might have done something about it. There seems to have been a complete lack of communication and misunderstanding all along the line, because Zo and I were told that we could not repatriate the body for ten years. No mention was made of what you've just told me. Our original intention was to bring him back to France and bury him in the Foreign Legion's cemetery; I know it's what he wanted. We thought it pointless to go through the exercise so many years later, so we both decided to leave him in peace there.

Zo was the elder of the two and gone by the time that ten-year period was over anyway.'

I expect the shock of what she had just heard then led her to say something that she might not have otherwise said in my presence. 'I am sure that, if there had not been such a complete collapse of everything, we would have got back together.'

If..., I thought it was one of the most depressing words in any language.

Chapter 21

FURTHER REVELATIONS

A longish queue of patrons waited to pay for their purchases in the smart Parisian pastry shop and tearoom on the Champs-Elysées. The original fin-de-siècle décor cannot have changed much, or very little, since it first opened. Upstairs, the feeling of being transported back in time was even more marked, as the room was well-insulated from the roar of traffic on the Champs-Elysées below; seated up here, one expected to see Leslie Caron floating in at any moment, elegantly turned out as Gigi. It was a fitting setting in which to discover more about the people I was here to talk of: Hélène and particularly Zulu. At a table by a window, a woman with finely chiselled features and a handsome man sat side by side. Much as I had expected, neither was young, both probably well in their seventies, if not older. Well, that was hardly surprising; Zulu would have been in his late nineties now and these were his younger cousins.

My companion, an erstwhile minister who had served under Mohammed Reza Shah, spotted them and led me in their direction, greeting her, calling her *Mali-jaan*, before turning to

The Fourth Wife of Aliyar Bey

her brother. Introductions were made and orders placed. I was here to meet Malek and Ilkhan Zelli, Zulu's Aunt Shouket's children, who had agreed to meet me. I would hear about the Zulgadars, more about Zulu himself, and about a younger Hélène, who had worked not very far from here in her days as a model with Mme Colbert. I was agog with anticipation at the thought of meeting other people who had known him well. This was an initiative I had undertaken independently and would provide corroboration, which I wanted as much for myself, even if it was too late for the record. After all these years, I was sure Hélène would be interested to have news of Ilkhan, of whom she had been fond.

I would come away that afternoon in confusion and resolved to absorb this new information before presenting it to Mathilde and eventually to Hélène. It was too late for their book, but it would change what we three knew and believed, of Zulu, of his life and his origins.

I recounted the story of my futile search for the grave and when asked whether he knew the location of Zulu's grave, Ilkhan assured me he did, that there was indeed a grave; his cousin was buried in the Foreign Legion's cemetery near Marseille, just as he would have wished. Both Ilkhan and Felix Aghayan had been approached for a contribution at the time of Zulu's death. He smiled when I described my absurd quest in Spain, and I expressed my satisfaction at knowing there was a logical explanation; Hélène would be pleased to hear of this. I knew that the cemetery of which he spoke would be in Aubagne, near Marseille, where the Foreign Legion had established its headquarters after leaving Algeria. Curious to hear the cousins' version on the history of the family, I brought up their oil holdings and was nonplussed to be told that there had been none. Not sure that I had understood, I echoed, 'None?'

'None,' he replied.

A glimmer of understanding on my part – he was too polite to say what Hélène was reported to have said, that Zulu was embroidering events beyond recognition. Perhaps the version he told her, which, naturally, she had from him was just the kind of fabulating that had so dismayed her? In my bewilderment, I still had time to marvel at the potency of a lie that had lasted fifty or more years; it was in print now, and I had contributed, however modestly, to its perpetuation.

Ilkhan had more to say about the Zulgadars of the past. 'Our forefathers were landowners and horse breeders of high repute; already well-established before the arrival of the Ottomans in the fifteenth century, and their power grew under the new rulers.'

There followed a story that I did not entirely understand, about a daughter given in marriage by one member of the family, in spite of the disapproval of another. This seemed to have caused a rift that could not be healed. I did gather that the offended man and his family left Azerbaijan and went to Isfahan, which was then beginning to acquire importance

The Fourth Wife of Aliyar Bey

and fame under the Safavids. While I was still struggling to absorb this new information, Ilkhan continued with a story about his grandfather, Alayar, who had attended the Exposition Universelle, a world's fair held in Paris in 1900.

'He wore his *tcherkesska*[30] when he went out in the streets. It caused such a furore that crowds of people followed him; the police had to be called in, and they requested him not to wear it in public.'

If Ilkhan bore any resemblance to his grandfather, I was more inclined to believe that a fine-looking exotic man of impressive looks and bearing would attract the interest of a crowd, particularly if his costume was unusual too.

This same grandfather was governor of the province in which they lived on an estate he'd named Alahbad. He and his household came to grief after the Russian takeover of the country. A Russian, newly appointed to oversee the province, ordered Alayar to cut down a grove of oaks on his land. Alayar refused, explaining his reason; their presence prevented flooding and soil erosion. The Russian, certainly an administrator but certainly not a man who understood the land, took exception to his orders being questioned and took recourse to the usual solution of ignorant men come by chance to power. He sent the family before a firing squad. Fortunately, Ali, Mahrokh, and their children had already fled the country and Ali's two sisters were away, being already married.

---

[30] Tcherkasska/Tcherkesska: a kneelength coat belted wih a sash.

Ilkhan could not know what I had been told. Nor had he a reason to invent these stories. The siblings had no idea that a book about their cousin's life had just been published. Neither had they known that Hélène now lived in France. I was struck by the extreme courtesy and dignified bearing of them both. What a pity it was time to leave. I left them with Hélène's address, and we parted with effusive thanks on my part and polite reminders from them to convey their regards to her if I should speak to her before they could write.

My Parisian hosts probably found me dull company for the rest of the evening, as I struggled to reconcile two very different accounts. For several months I had been so caught up in the story that it took me a few days to conclude that it was not my responsibility, that I was doing no more than conveying information not falsifying it; here was no question of malice or an ulterior motive.

I still felt uncomfortable at being the one to bring, once again, knowledge that might wound. For me, revealing the truth at all costs and under any circumstances that had never been a convincing argument in the past and was not now. This particular revelation could not be concealed but it did not make me relish my role any more or mitigate the effect of what I was about to disclose – namely, that Hélène had been lied to consistently by the man she had lived with for over twenty years.

The Fourth Wife of Aliyar Bey

Neither had I any idea how Mathilde would react, but it was she who would have to be told first. I rang her at her flat in Paris and then at La Métairie, hoping to find her at one or the other. No reply; best to phone again the next day. In the meantime, I wondered whether I should have left well enough alone; my well-intentioned curiosity had put me in an unenviable situation. Mathilde might be no more than intrigued by this new twist to the tale, perhaps rue the fact that it was too late to incorporate it in the book, but how would Hélène react?

Mathilde's voice was uncharacteristically subdued when I reached her at La Métairie after a couple of days. Hélène had been found in her bed two days earlier. It was supposed that death had occurred sometime during the previous day. The postman had called with a letter requiring her signature and noticed two cats sitting on the windowsill, waiting to be let in. After a few minutes passed with no reply, he thought it best to alert the neighbours before continuing on his round. I sat numb with surprise, unable to work out whether I was relieved that she would not have to digest a completely new story.

Mathilde continued, 'She was not in robust health, but I think the loneliness and sense of being abandoned was even more acute as the years went on… You are aware that she was hitting the bottle quite enthusiastically, aren't you? Had been for some years.'

About the bottle? I'd suspected as much, but no, I had not known for certain. It came as no surprise though, and I still had not told her why I had rung. *So composed*, I thought, though I was sure that losing a friend of many years must have affected her more than she would allow to show.

'I'll come for the weekend after I've finished this job next week,' I said before ringing off.

And so I returned to La Métairie.

After I had told Mathilde of my meeting with the Zellis, her only observation was that she understood now what Hélène had meant about Aliyar's fanciful stories. Neither of us could fathom why an already rich and colourful story should be thus distorted. For instance, we wondered, what was the purpose of claiming the origin of the Zulgadars to be in Baghdad? Weren't Azerbaijan and the events there exotic enough?

'Too late to do anything about it, so it will just have to remain yet another untold story until some other purveyor of tales decides to take it up. Yves goes to Marseille on a project, and I'll see whether he can take me to the cemetery – it would be too much to ask of you again! Don't fret about it, my dear. The book's already out, and this will be a last tribute to my friendship with Hélène. After that, it's time to let it rest.'

***

It was cooler the next time I was in Málaga. I was able to excuse myself from a game of bridge at Luis's, as I do not play. Instead, I took a taxi to the cemetery. I was drawn back even though I now knew that there was nothing in it for me to find and why that was really so. I would look out over the sea to Morocco where Zulu had spent time and it seemed a suitable place to reflect upon and remember both these women, one dead, the other still alive; the sadness on Hélène's face at our last meeting in the little grey house; and her words on the tape when she told me of her first meeting with Zulu – 'I felt as if I had been branded. I recalled Mathilde asking me whether I would really want to read a polemic by a politician and then thought of Mathilde and Hélène's decision to record what they had known and seen and their belief that the record mattered, I believed and hoped it did matter.

My own role in their project had been a minor one, but it had left me breathless, as if I had been tossed in a boat down a tumultuous river. I puzzled over the effect upon me of somebody long dead and so far removed from my life. Coming into direct contact with the man must have been like touching an electrified fence. It irked me however that I had still not penetrated the enigma which was Zulu; it was doubtful that anyone ever would.

Soon there would be nobody left alive who remembered him. All that would remain of Aliyar was this account, if anyone cared to read it. For our different reasons, the three of us had wanted for him a memorial with more impact than a headstone in a cemetery nobody would visit, and I did not know whether we had achieved that.

At any rate, there would be no other obituary for the boy who fled Azerbaijan.

Printed in Great Britain
by Amazon.co.uk, Ltd.,
Marston Gate.